Previously published as part of

'The Big Book of Soft Toys'

Also available in this series

FRAMING
MACRAMÉ
RUGMAKING
POTTERY
WEAVING
JEWELLERY
CANDLEMAKING
CROCHET
APPLIQUÉ
SOFT TOYS
COUNTRY CRAFTS

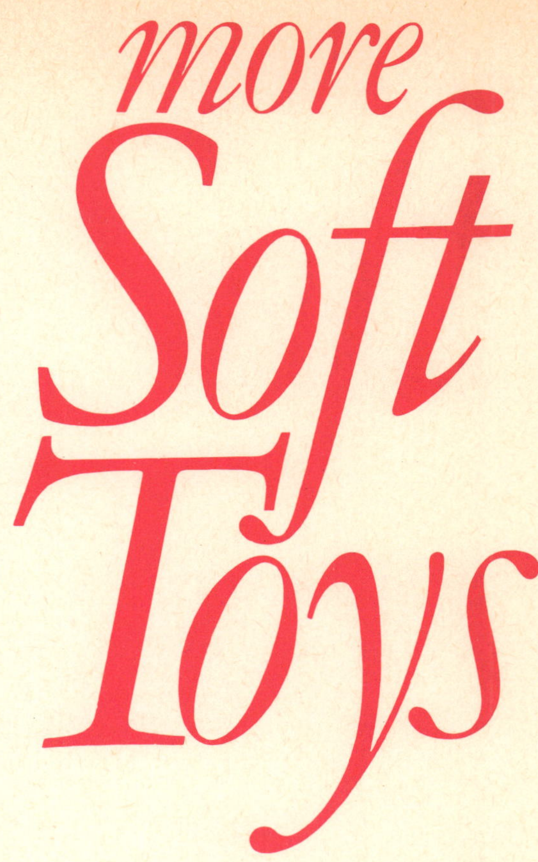

Previously published as part of
'The Big Book of Soft Toys'

MABS TYLER

photographs by Gina Harris
line illustrations by John Kingsford

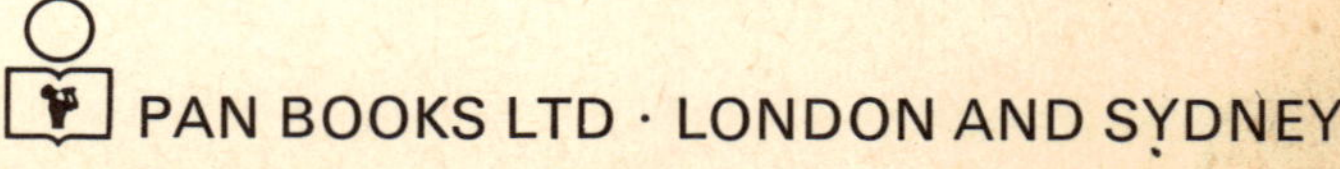
PAN BOOKS LTD · LONDON AND SYDNEY

First published 1972 as part of *The Big Book of Soft Toys*
by Wolfe Publishing Ltd
This edition published 1974 by Pan Books Ltd,
Cavaye Place, London SW10 9PG

ISBN 0 330 24242 3

TO ANGELA

Printed by Cripplegate Printing Co. Ltd., Edenbridge, England

Contents

Chapter Five. Gifts to make

Introduction

SINCE BEFORE recorded memory the making of toys has been among the most satisfying of domestic accomplishments.

The most popular of all toys, from then until now, has been the one which was right for the child for whom it was designed.

Soft Toys offers a range of toys which, while not demanding a skill beyond that of the average aunt, mother or grandmother, contains something which will please most children.

Many of the toys, in fact, are simple enough in design for quite young children to make for themselves. And these simple shapes can be turned into something more decorative and elaborate by colourful embroidery.

Before starting to make any of the toys it is important to read the General Hints given below.

Acknowledgements

Many thanks must be given to friends and students for practical help with drawings, sewing and checking, and to all who gave encouragement and showed interest in the book's progress.

General Hints

READ ALL INSTRUCTIONS FULLY BEFORE STARTING TO MAKE A TOY

Patterns when cut out in thin card (templates) are easier to trace round, and they last longer.
Mark on each template (a) the number of pieces to be cut from it, (b) any directions for sewing.
Keep all the templates for each toy fastened together. Place the biggest templates on the fabric first.
Cut out all the necessary pieces for the toy before starting to sew it.
Keep all the pieces for the toy together in a bag.
Embroider only simple designs on any small parts.
When sewing the parts together check that all decorated sides will be on the outside of the toy, e.g. balls, dice.
Be careful to pair right and left sides, especially when embroidering, e.g. animal sides, wings.
Leave openings for stuffing in the least noticeable places.
Use stuffing in small, soft pieces to make a smooth toy.
Do not overfill slither toys, or they may be too heavy to play with easily.
Have no hanging pieces, loose decoration or long embroidery stitches on toys designed to be much handled.
When sewing stockinette or other similar 'stretchy' fabric, use a longer stitch, preferably a back stitch, to give elasticity.
Tack fur and fur fabric and long-piled fabric on the wrong side with small stitches, leaving the stitches in for added strength.

Grid System

The pattern for each toy is overlaid by a blue grid. Each square on this grid represents 2.5 cm (1"). To transfer the pattern, draw a grid of 2.5 cm (1") squares. On this grid mark with dots where the lines of the drawing cross the lines of the blue grid.
There are two sizes of grid used in this book. The very small squares will have to be multiplied by 4, and the larger squares multiplied by 2 to bring them up to 2.5 cm (1"). You can, of course, make the toys larger than their intended size by drawing out your own grid of, say, 5 cm (2") squares.

Using felt

No allowance need be made for turnings because felt does not fray.
There is no 'right' or 'wrong' side.
Use a very sharply pointed pencil for tracing; never use ball-point pens or felt-tip pens.

Jemima Jane, a lovely Victorian Miss.
Instructions for making her are
given on page 59

Place pattern and fabric on a hard surface to give a clearer outline.
Use a white pencil or tailor's chalk on dark colours.
Keep the traced side as the wrong side when sewing the toy.
When cutting two matching pieces from a template, e.g. two sides of an animal, reverse the template or pattern when tracing the second piece so that the pencil marks on both pieces will be on the inside of the finished toy.
Cut inside the pencil lines to avoid grubby seams.
Always pin and tack close to the edge to avoid dirty marks.
When leaving work unfinished, stick needle under finished embroidery, or on the edge.
Mark the positions of features, etc, with tacking threads, *not* pencil.
To transfer a design for embroidering, trace the design on to thin paper, place it in position on the felt and work small running stitches in a contrasting colour through both paper and felt, afterwards tearing away the paper. The running stitches can be pulled out when the embroidery is finished.
Do not pull embroidery stitches too tight or the felt will pucker.
Sewing can be done on the right side.

Using fabric

Trace round the template on to the wrong side of the fabric and cut 1.25 cm ($\frac{1}{2}$") outside the line to allow for turnings.
When cutting two matching pieces from a template, e.g. two sides of an animal, reverse the template for the second piece so that the wrong side of the material will be on the inside of the toy.
Sew or stitch on the pencil line.
After sewing trim off the surplus seam allowance.
Snip 'v's out of all curves.
Snip into all corners as close to the stitching as possible to keep seams flat.
Use fabric with a firm, close weave. Loosely woven fabric, unless it is lined, will not keep in the stuffing.
Tack the pieces together outside the stitching line.
Practise sewing doll's features on paper or fabric cut to the same size as the doll's face before drawing or embroidering on to the toy.

Useful things to have

Sharp cutting-out scissors.
Scissors for cutting paper and card.
Small, very sharply pointed scissors.
A selection of needles.
Wire nippers.
Stuffing sticks – a blunted pencil, blunted wooden skewer, blunted orange stick, blunted cocktail stick.
Very sharp pencils, black and white, or white tailor's chalk.
Felt-tip pens – black, red, brown, blue.
Transparent thread.
Tape measure.
Ruler.
A pair of compasses.
Masking tape.
Colourless upholstery adhesive.
Thin card.
Tracing paper.
Piece box containing remnants and scraps of various fabrics, lace, fur, fur fabric, old nylon stockings, suede or kid gloves, Christmas ribbons and cords, sequins, beads, foam rubber, pipe cleaners.

Terms

Gingham – closely woven, thin cotton material, generally in a variety of checked and striped patterns.
Courtelle – fluffy-pile, man-made jersey fabric, used for dressing gowns.
Vilene – man-made compressed fibre, used for interlining; in various thicknesses, does not fray.
Fusible Vilene can be ironed on to fabrics as a backing, so preventing any fraying.
Wadding – compressed cotton fibres, enclosed in a very thin skin to make a flat padding.
Tarlatan – stiffened, loosely woven cotton material, used to make stiff ballet tutus.
Calico – firmly woven, strong cotton material, white or unbleached (sheeting).
Crash – coarsely woven, unbleached linen, very strong.
Cambric – finely woven, soft cotton material, used for handkerchiefs.
Poplin – firmly woven cotton material with smooth, semi-shiny surface.
Kapok – fluffy, loose fibres, used for stuffing.
Ricrac braid – decorative braid in which threads are pulled tighter on one side, giving it a wavy line.

Velcro – a type of fastener comprising two pieces, one with hooks and the other with loops, which hold firmly when pressed together.
Masking tape – an adhesive, strong paper tape.
Dowel rod – thin, hard, round wooden rod.
Felt-tip pens – marker pens with an ink reservoir, thin fibre tips for fine work and thick felt tips for broader outlines.
Pipe cleaner chenille – a continuous length (up to ten feet) of thin, pliable wire encased in a fluffy, thick covering.
Dolly pegs – old-fashioned wooden clothes pegs cut in one piece, with a round knob and two legs.
Lurex thread – a fine metal thread in gold, silver and colours.

Stitches

Running stitch

can be used for seaming together two pieces of thin or medium thicknesses of fabric or, with added variations, as a decorative stitch. Work from left to right, putting the needle in and out in one motion and keeping the spaces the same size as the stitches.

Variations on running stitch

Whipped. Thread through each running stitch in the same direction to give a corded effect.
Double whipped. Work two rows of threading, the second one in the opposite direction from the first one.
Threaded. Thread up through one stitch and down through the next one.
Double threaded. Two rows of threading are worked, the second one in the opposite direction to the first.
Block running. Rows of running stitches are worked with stitches exactly above each other. These can be threaded and double threaded, whipped and double whipped. A check design is obtained if rows of three stitches are worked with the second rows of blocks in the spaces underneath the first row and so on.

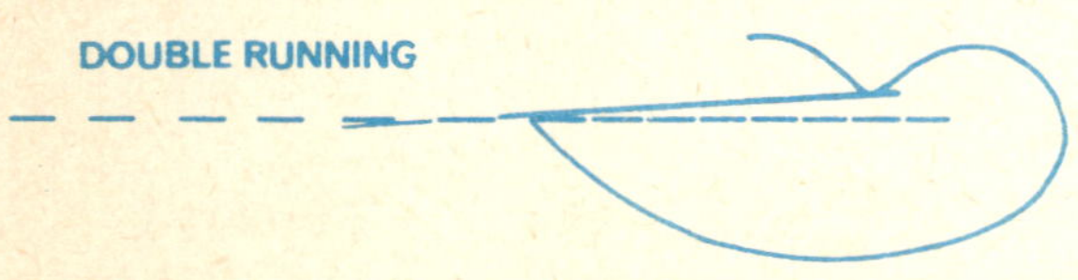

Double running. Work a second row of running stitches on top of the first row so that the second row of stitches fill in the spaces in between the stitches of the first row. This can be used as an alternative to back stitch.

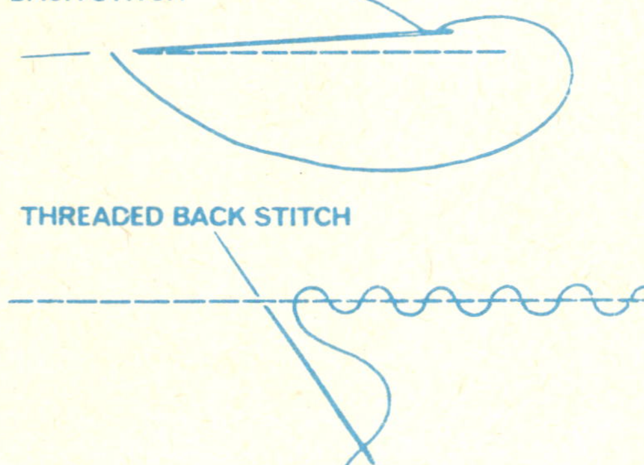

Back stitch. Work one running stitch. Insert the needle into the same hole, bringing it out a stitch's length to the left. Continue, working back into each previous stitch, completely filling the space. Back stitch can be threaded and double threaded, whipped and double whipped.
Chain stitch. Bring the thread out on the right side of the work and hold it under the left thumb. Put the needle back into the same hole, bringing it out again over the held thread. Do not pull the thread too tight. This stitch can be whipped and threaded.

WHIPPED CHAIN – can also be threaded

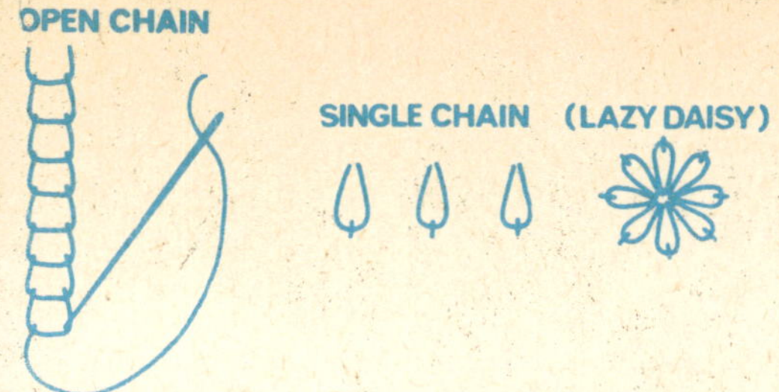

Open chain stitch. This is formed in the same way as chain stitch, but the needle is inserted to the right of the first stitch and slanted to the left, to come out under the first stitch. Keep the loop loose enough to take the second stitch.

Fly stitch. This too is a form of open chain stitch. Hold the thread under the left thumb and insert the needle to the right of the first stitch, bringing it out lower down in the middle of the two stitches and over the loop. Insert the needle under the loop to hold it, bringing it out to the left under the first stitch. This stitch can be done horizontally, vertically and singly as a filling stitch.

Snail trail or coral stitch. Hold thread horizontally under left thumb. Take a slanting stitch to the left through the material and including the held thread. Gently pull up to form a knot, and repeat the process.

Buttonhole stitch. Work from left to right. Hold the thread to the right under the left thumb. Insert the needle about 3mm ($\frac{1}{8}$") above the hole, bringing it out close to the hole and over the held thread. Pull the thread to hold the loop and hold it under the thumb again. Insert the needle in line and to the right of the last stitch, bringing it out under the insertion point in line with the first stitch and over the held thread. The stitches should be at right angles to the row of loops.

Pointed buttonhole. As for buttonhole, but three buttonhole stitches are made into each hole; in the first one the needle slants down to the left, the second stitch is vertical and in the third the needle slants down to the right.

Stem stitch. Work from left to right. It is similar to back stitch in reverse, the needle brought out halfway along the last stitch and touching it, giving a corded effect.

Couching. A cord or several threads are held in position by working vertical stitches over them, close to each side of the threads.

Herring bone. Worked on two parallel lines from left to right. Bring the thread out on the top line. Take a stitch from right to left on the bottom line so that the thread slopes down to the right. Take the next stitch in the top line so that the thread slopes up to the right, crossing the previous thread.

Cross stitch. Worked on two lines. Work a row of stitches sloping from left to right between the two lines. A second row worked in the opposite direction using the same holes crosses over the first row of threads.

Joining stitches

Oversewing. Work from right to left. Hold the two edges of the material together and insert the needle at right angles from back to front through both thicknesses. Continue so, keeping the spaces even, so that the stitches will slant evenly.

Crossed oversewing is obtained by working a second row from left to right, using the same holes.

Double-locking oversewing. Work as for oversewing, but taking two stitches into each hole, so that the slanting stitch and the straight stitch from the same hole give a zigzag effect.

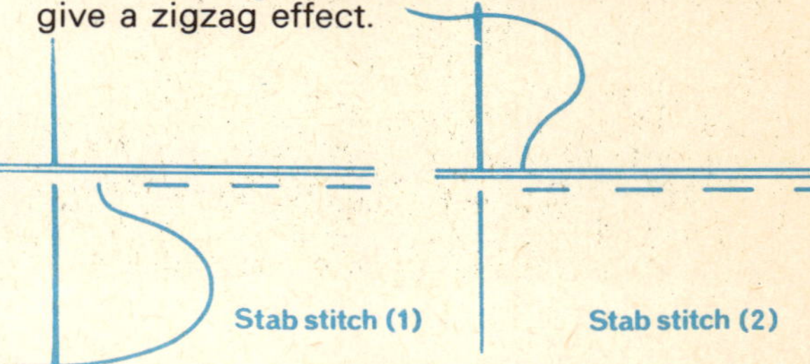

Stab stitch. This is used when joining two thick fabrics such as felt, so that one piece is not stretched more than the other, as it would be if running stitch were used. The effect is like running stitch. Insert the needle at right angles to the edges of material from front to back and then from back to front.

Fishbone stitch. This stitch makes a flat seam, not ridged as in oversewing. Place the two pieces of material with the edges butting on each other and touching. Work from right to left and take a stitch from back to front first in one piece and then in the other.

Ladder stitch. This is another flat seam join. Lay the two pieces of material with edges butting against each other. Take a small stitch parallel to the edges first in one piece and then in the other. Pull the thread firmly but not tight enough to pucker the material.

Laced buttonhole. Work buttonhole stitch on the edges of both pieces of material. Lay the two buttonholed edges butting on each other. Lace the edges together by sewing through the loops on each edge.

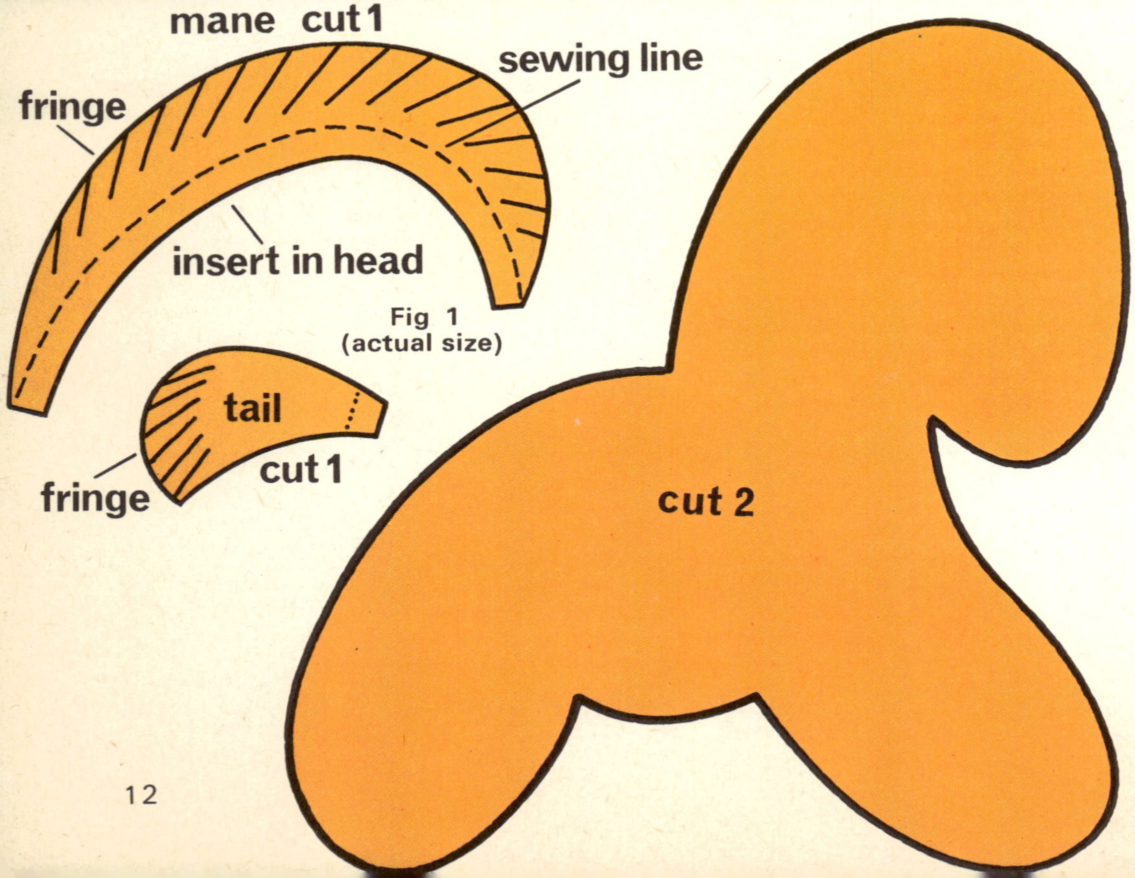

mane cut 1

sewing line

fringe

insert in head

Fig 1
(actual size)

tail

cut 1

fringe

cut 2

CHAPTER ONE

Decorated toys

Mobiles

Mobiles are attractive, not just for any colour or interesting shape they may have, but because they have movement as well, and this, like tropical fish in a tank, or flying birds, holds attention and interest. Mobiles can be gay and exotic with birds or butterflies or dragonflies; comical with faces and masks; abstract with wood or wire shapes; even musical with metal shapes or figures.

A mobile merry-go-round

Here are gaily coloured little horses and cocks swinging round under a circus ring-like top, bright with embroidery and sparkling with sequins and beads. They are cut in two pieces without a gusset and joined together to make flattish figures. There are three cocks and three horses, all in different colours.

You will need:

Fairly small pieces of many different-coloured felts, for cutting the bodies (here the horses are sky blue, orange, mauve, and the cocks royal blue, rose pink and emerald green); small scraps of other colours in felt for manes and tails, legs and wings; a larger piece in one colour for the ring they are swinging on; embroidery silks; sequins; beads; metal thread; kapok or similar for stuffing; some thick cardboard, a piece of firm wire about 63 cm (25″) long and some gilt cord.

Horses

The template for the little horses is in three pieces, for body, tail and mane (Fig 1). Cut two body pieces, one mane and tail in a different shade. Reverse the template always when tracing the second body piece and cut inside the pencil lines to avoid a grubby-looking seam on pale colours.

Embroider the pieces before sewing together. Work a line of chain stitch in embroidery silk all round the outline of the horse, about 6 mm (¼″) in from the edge (Fig 2). Over this sew continuous fly stitch in bright metal-thread. Sew a sequin at the end of it on the forehead. The eye is a curved line of silver chain stitch with straight stitches raying out from it. In the centre of the triangle of embroidery formed by legs and neck sew a fairly large sequin, with three lines of silver fly stitch pointing in to the legs and neck. Sew a sequin at the end of each.

Embroider the second piece for the other side.

Cut the round end of the tail piece in a fringe and pin it on to one body piece so that it sticks out jauntily (Fig 3).

The mane is cut in a curve to follow the line of the head and stretches from just above the eye to the base of the neck. Fringe the edge and pin in place on the same side piece. Place the two body pieces together with right sides outside, placing pins carefully through the embroidery so that they won't leave marks on the felt.

Oversew the edges, starting from the chin, up the head to the beginning of the mane. Sew in the mane with the head seam using stab stitch, inserting the needle at right angles from front to back through the three thicknesses of felt and then inserting at right angles from back to front through the mane only and close to the edge of the head felt. When finished, it will resemble the oversewing.

Sew to the base of the neck. Stuff the head with small pieces of stuffing, keeping it smooth and softly rounded. Continue sewing round the back leg, and then ease the stuffing in place with a blunt pencil end. Sew up the back seam of the front leg and about half of the front seam, and then stuff the rest of the body. Sew up the opening.

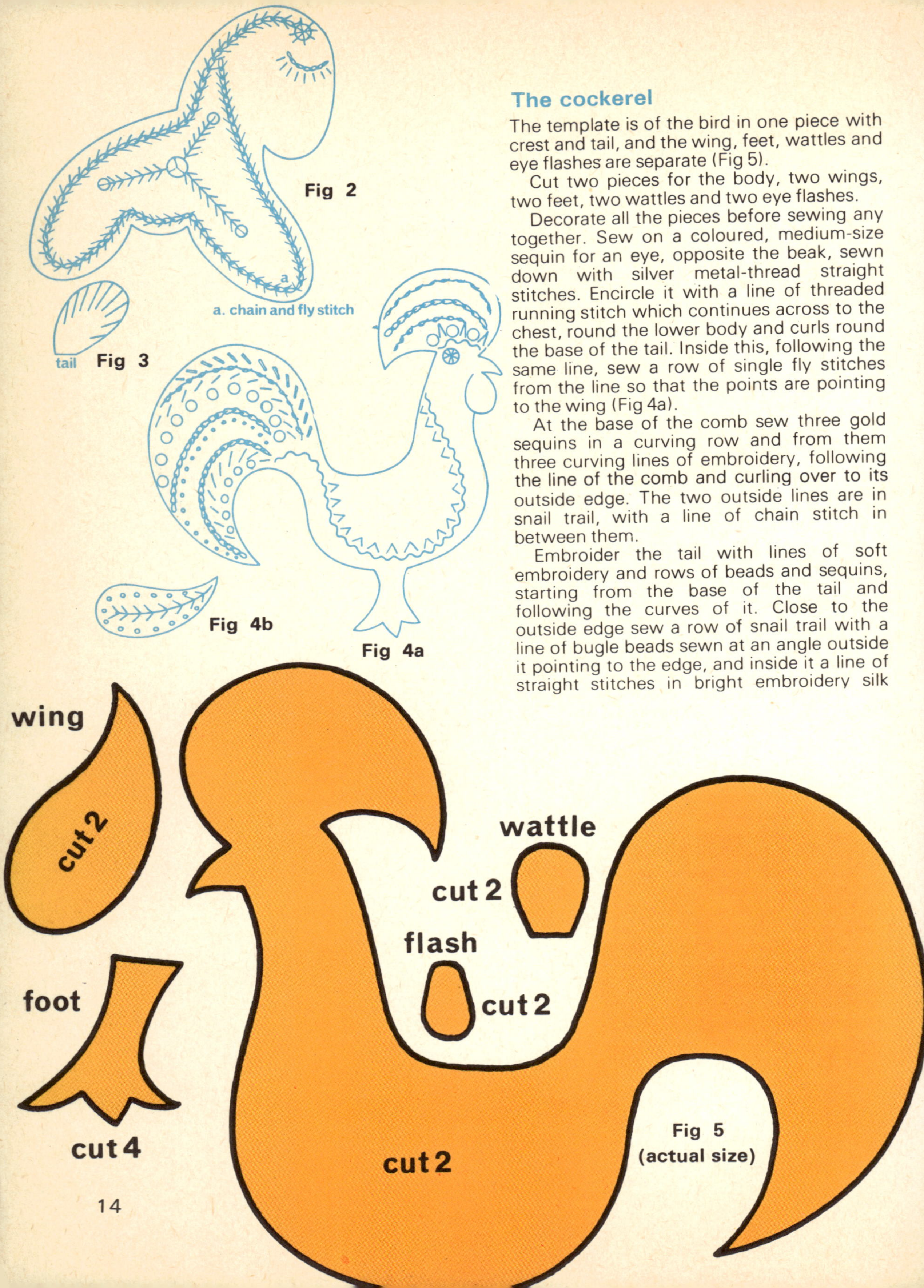

Fig 2

Fig 3

Fig 4a

Fig 4b

Fig 5 (actual size)

The cockerel

The template is of the bird in one piece with crest and tail, and the wing, feet, wattles and eye flashes are separate (Fig 5).

Cut two pieces for the body, two wings, two feet, two wattles and two eye flashes.

Decorate all the pieces before sewing any together. Sew on a coloured, medium-size sequin for an eye, opposite the beak, sewn down with silver metal-thread straight stitches. Encircle it with a line of threaded running stitch which continues across to the chest, round the lower body and curls round the base of the tail. Inside this, following the same line, sew a row of single fly stitches from the line so that the points are pointing to the wing (Fig 4a).

At the base of the comb sew three gold sequins in a curving row and from them three curving lines of embroidery, following the line of the comb and curling over to its outside edge. The two outside lines are in snail trail, with a line of chain stitch in between them.

Embroider the tail with lines of soft embroidery and rows of beads and sequins, starting from the base of the tail and following the curves of it. Close to the outside edge sew a row of snail trail with a line of bugle beads sewn at an angle outside it pointing to the edge, and inside it a line of straight stitches in bright embroidery silk worked at the same angle. A line of sequins follows the same curve. Under this is a row of chain stitch with small gold beads alongside it. Next, sew a line of metal-thread chain stitch with straight stitches angled from it, finished off with a row of gold sequins.

Decorate the wings with a line of fly stitch in embroidery silk, down the centre, with small bright beads all round it (Fig 4b).

Oversew two foot pieces together for each foot, starting from the leg and stuffing each claw as it is sewn with tiny pieces of kapok, easing it in very carefully with a blunted cocktail stick.

Pin the foot in place on one of the side pieces. Pin the two side pieces together with right sides outside, matching beaks, crests and tails.

Start sewing from under the beak, over the crest and halfway along the under seam of the crest. Stuff the tiny beak carefully, easing stuffing into the point, and stuff the head and the point of the crest. Sew the rest of the under seam, and on down the back of the neck, over the tail and a short way along the under seam of the tail. Ease stuffing gently into the point of the tail and continue sewing a little and stuffing all round the rest of the seams up to the beak. Stuff carefully and not too hard, but firmly at the two narrowest places at neck and base of tail, to prevent the head and tail drooping.

Sew a red wattle each side of the head under the beak, sewing one side of it to the head and the other hanging free.

Sew the two eye flashes (Fig 6) under the eye just behind the wattles.

Sew a wing in place on each side with the point of it close to the back seam.

Thread a needle with a fine transparent nylon thread and thread it into their backs to find the correct suspension place for the cocks and horses. The one for the cock seems to be at the most outward-curving point of the tail, almost opposite the point of the comb, and for the little horses about halfway along the mane. Move the thread slightly from place to place until the figure balances.

For merry-go-round frame

Cut six pieces of thick card 10 cm (4") long and 4 cm (1½") wide. Cut three equal scallops along one long side (Fig 7). Use each card as a template for its two pieces of felt, reversing the template to trace the

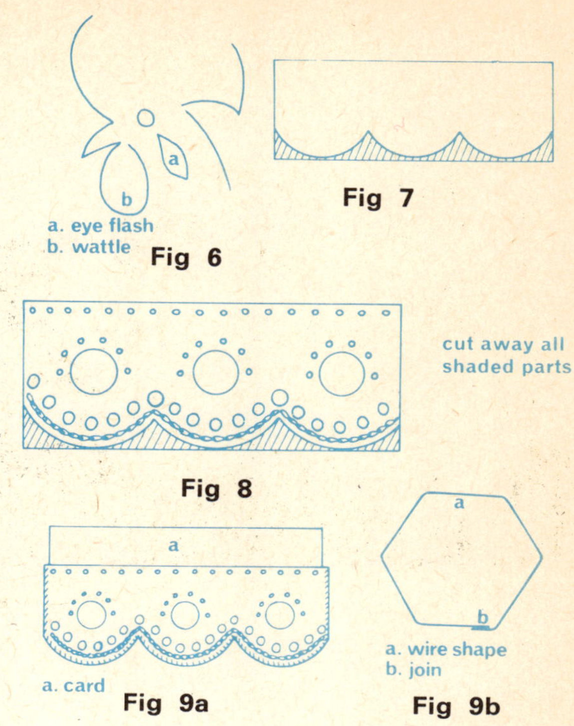

Fig 6

Fig 7

Fig 8

Fig 9a

Fig 9b

second piece and keeping the pencilled side for the wrong side. Mark each card with its corresponding felts; keeping them together will ensure a good fit, as each card can vary a little.

Embroider one piece of felt from each pair with a line of silver metal-thread chain stitch near the edge and a line of sequins inside it, following the line of the scallops (Fig 8). Sew a large sequin in the centre of the curve with small gold beads sewn round the top half of it. Sew a close row of gold beads along the top edge.

Sew the two pieces of felt together, a plain piece and an embroidered piece, on the right sides, sewing the two short sides and the scalloped edge. Insert the appropriate card and sew up the long edge (Fig 9a). Repeat this with the other five sections.

Sew all six together in a hexagon shape by oversewing their short sides together firmly. Sew more sequins up over the joins to match those round the scallop.

On the inside, on two hexagon points, opposite to each other, sew a length of gilt cord to suspend the frame.

Take the 63 cm (25") length of firm wire, and with pliers bend it into a hexagon shape (Fig 9b) to fit inside the frame. The two ends

a. nylon thread
b. dowel rod
c. fruit box

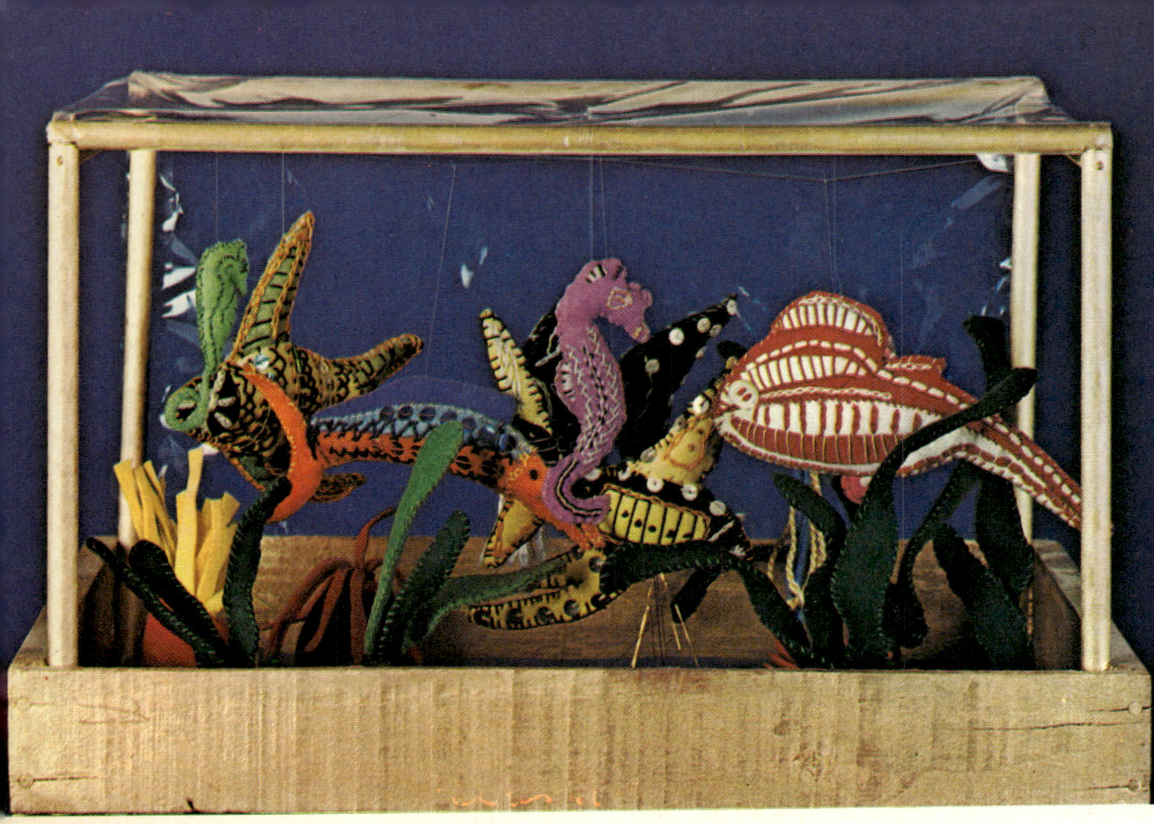

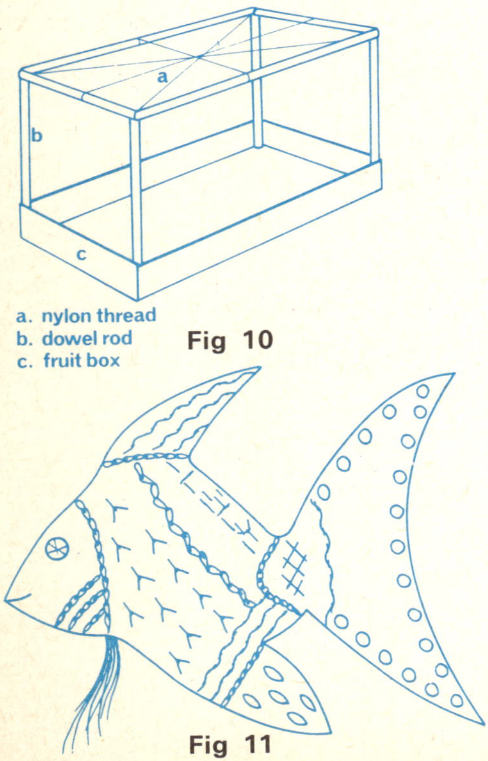

Fig 10

Fig 11

should overlap a little. Bind or solder the two ends in place. Cut a 60 cm (24'') length of felt 1.25 cm (½'') wide and sew it round the wire to enclose it. Sew this on to the inside of the frame just below the top edge, keeping the sewn side of it tucked away close to the frame. This will keep the frame in rigid shape.

Thread small bugle beads on to the nylon thread sewn on to the horses' and cocks' backs, threading twice as many on to the cocks' threads as on the horses' (this will ensure that they hang at different levels). Sew the end of each thread into the angles of the hexagon, fastening off very securely, because nylon thread tends to be slippery.

An aquarium of felt fish

Colourful, exotic-looking, imaginative fish floating around in a waterless aquarium, and all of them handmade.

You will need:

Bright, many-coloured felts; embroidery silks; sequins; beads; fine metal-threads; an ordinary fruit or seed box, for the aquarium; some 9 mm (⅜'') dowel rod; some green and blue tarlatan; two or three sheets of Cellophane; some stuffing material; some nylon thread.

Make the aquarium first

The box should have sides about 4 cm (1½") high. Cut four pieces of dowel rod about 23 cm (9") high for a fruit box measuring 38 cm by 20 cm (15" by 8") and fix them firmly with nails or glue, standing upright in each corner of the box (Fig 10). Cut four more pieces of dowel, corresponding to the measurements of the two long and two short sides of the box, and nail or glue these to the tops of the corner rods, to form a frame. The frame looks rather splendid if sprayed with gold paint.

Tie fine nylon thread across the top from corner to corner and from side to side across the middle. The fish will hang from these.

The fish

Now for the fish to go in it. These can be long and thin; fat and stubby; flat; ordinary fishy shapes with exaggerated fins, tails and scales; spotted; striped; with coloured bands which glow and flash with sequins, beads and fine metal-thread.

Go to a tropical fish shop or to the aquarium in a zoo to get some ideas, then add some decorations of your own. Here are some to start you off.

Some of the fish have bands of colour added to the shape. In other cases the fish template has been cut into sections and the pieces used to cut out the different colours; the sections are then sewn together with decorative stitching to make the original shape. You will find the templates at Fig 17.

A black and white angel fish

The black, white and silver fish is shaped rather like an angel fish with a crescent-shaped tail nearly as big as his body (Fig 11). He is embroidered with white embroidery silk and fine silver metal-thread on black felt.

Cut two shapes in felt from the template and embroider the pieces first, taking care to make them for left and right sides.

The embroidery is in stripes of zigzag chain stitch and threaded running stitch with single fly stitches to indicate scales; a sequin eye, sequins edging his tail and a fine, floating fringe of white silk cord and fine silver metal-thread completes him.

Sew the edges together on the right side, starting at the mouth, round the top fin and all of the tail.

Stuff the tail, not too hard, and the top fin.

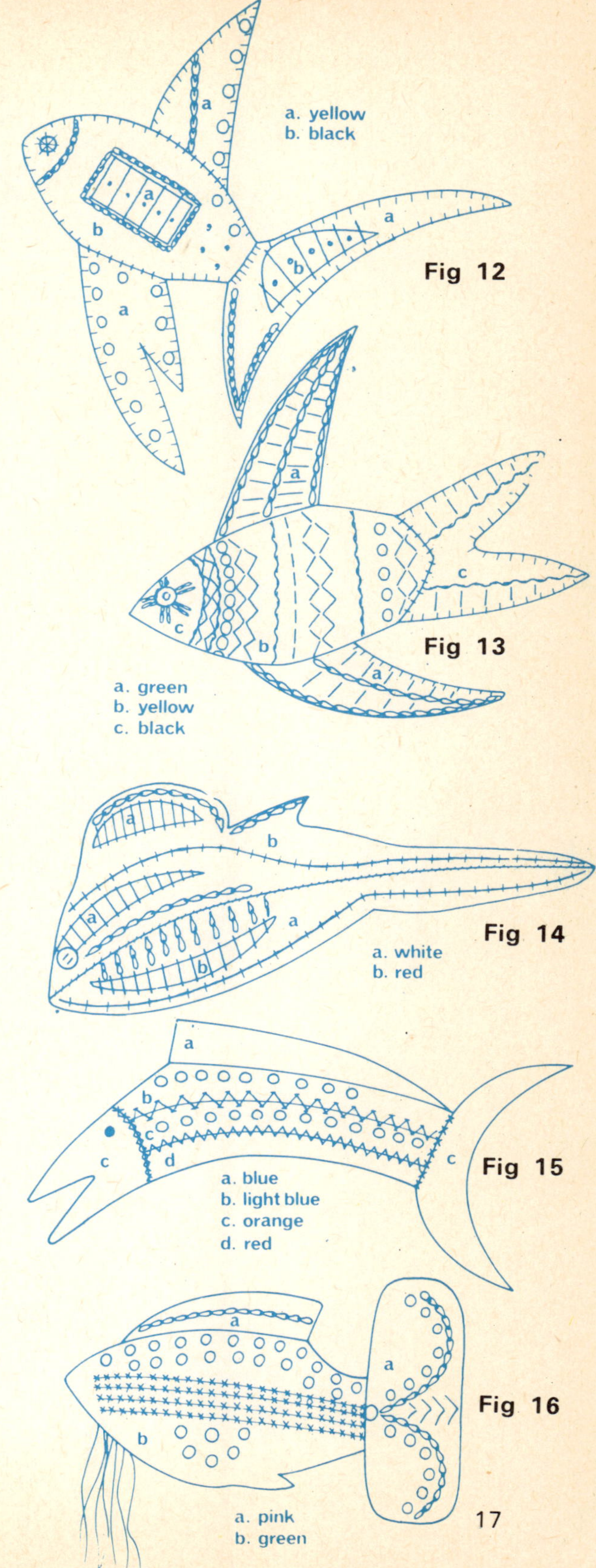

Fig 17a

Fig 17 (actual size)

Fig 17b

Continue the sewing, stuffing as you sew. Sew a fine nylon thread in his back, testing the placing of it so that he hangs straight and not tilted.

A shark-like angel fish

Another angel fish shape has a more shark-like tail and a forked lower fin (Fig 12). He is in black and yellow felt with black, orange and white embroidery. His body, fins and tail have been cut separately, the body in black felt and the fins and tail in yellow.

The body has a rectangle of yellow sewn on with long straight stitches in black and black french knots in the spaces, the whole surrounded with a line of orange chain stitch.

The tail has a triangle of black in the middle of each side, sewn with white straight stitches and white french knots.

The fins are joined with black buttonhole stitch, each sewn separately and stuffed, and then joined on to the main body with straight stitches. Sequins are sewn on the fins and along the body, a sequin for an eye and a gold metal-thread floating fringe from his fin.

A forked-tail angel fish

Another angel-type fish (Fig 13) has a narrowly forked tail; this time the body is in yellow felt and the fins and tail in bright green felt.

The head is in black felt, embroidered in a wheel design of bands of chain stitch in white and green, round a circular eye of two rings of chain stitch, in green and white.

The body is thickly embroidered with bands of double fly stitch in black, and black and orange whipped running stitch; in between them are bands of green and gold sequins and green bugle beads.

The fins are barred with black straight stitches held down by a band of orange chain stitch down the edges and the middle.

The tail is decorated with threaded running stitch and the entire edges are sewn together with black buttonhole stitch, the parts joined with black straight stitch.

A hump-backed fish

This fish (Fig 14) has a long, drooping tail and is very bright and quite grand in red and white. The template is cut in half from nose to tail, the upper half cut in red and the lower half in white felt. The two pieces are oversewn together.

The top half is decorated with curved bands of white felt held down with long straight stitches in red, with a thick white embroidery cotton couched down its length from its pearl button eye to the tail.

The lower half has a crescent-shaped piece of red felt sewn down with white stitches and, above it, vertical stripes of red chain stitch along its length. Below it is a couched line of thick red embroidery cotton from mouth to tail.

The long, thin, graceful fish

He has a body in three bars of colour, red, orange, blue, with a long, upstanding, darker blue fin stretching the full length of the body, a wicked-looking, beaked mouth and wide, crescent-shaped tail in bright orange (Fig 15).

The body colours are joined with black herring-bone stitch, with a line of royal blue sequins on the blue band and bright pink sequins on the orange band. Head and tail are joined to the body with paler orange cross stitch.

The hammer head

The last fish (Fig 16) is a very gay fellow. He has a body of bright green felt with a fin and a great hammer-shaped tail of pink. He looks as though he could be related to a hammer-head shark. From nose to tail his body has close bands of embroidered cross stitch and whipped running stitch in black and deep pink, with bands of green and gold sequins over it, and a semi-circle of blue and red sequins below. The pink fin has a line of green chain stitch along its length. The bold tail has two rows of green chain stitch curling out from the middle to the two ends, with lines of pink sequins following them and yellow fly stitches in between. The edges are buttonholed in green silk and the barbels under his chin are of fine golden metal-thread and bright blue cord.

Two little seahorses

They complete this fish family. One in mauve felt is embroidered in green, gold and black herring-bone and straight stitch and couching. A baby one in pale green felt is decorated with blue and fine green metal-thread chain stitch.

A crab (Fig 17b) in light brown felt with orange-coloured legs and claws, crawls on the bottom among the anemones (Fig 17b)

in red with waving yellow fronds and in green with red fronds.

A few embroidered pebbles among some strands of green felt seaweed (Fig 17a), (wavy shapes of green felt sewn round lengths of wire with their ends in modelling clay). Now the aquarium inhabitants are complete.

Line the bottom of the box with a layer of blue and of green tarlatan. Space the fish on the nylon threads across the frame and arrange the seaweed on the bottom. Cut Cellophane to fit right round the frame and stick it in place with adhesive. Cover the top with a piece of blue tarlatan, or another rectangle of Cellophane.

A merry-go-round of birds

Five little birds in bright-coloured felt, made very gay with coloured embroidery, sequins and beads, hang on a small, doll-sized merry-go-round.

You will need:

Several small pieces of felt in a variety of gay colours for the birds' bodies, wings and topknots; a larger piece of yellow felt for the merry-go-round; some kapok; coloured embroidery silks; some fine metal-thread in one or two colours; sequins and beads; a piece of manilla or thin card; a wooden skewer; a large cotton reel.

The bird shape for the template is quite easy to draw—a small circle for the head and an oval shape for the body. Join the two with two curved lines for the neck, add a pointed beak to the circle at one side and a larger-pointed triangle for the tail on the oval at the opposite side (Fig 18). The templates for wing and topknot are separate and they can be varied for each bird.

Make the birds rounder in shape by sewing in a gusset under the body from beak to tail. When the body template has been drawn, measure the curve from under the beak to the tail and this will be the length of the gusset—it should be 1.25 to 2 cm (½" to ¾") wide in the middle, tapering to a point at each end.

Trace round the templates on to different-coloured felts for each of the five birds. Each one needs two body pieces, one

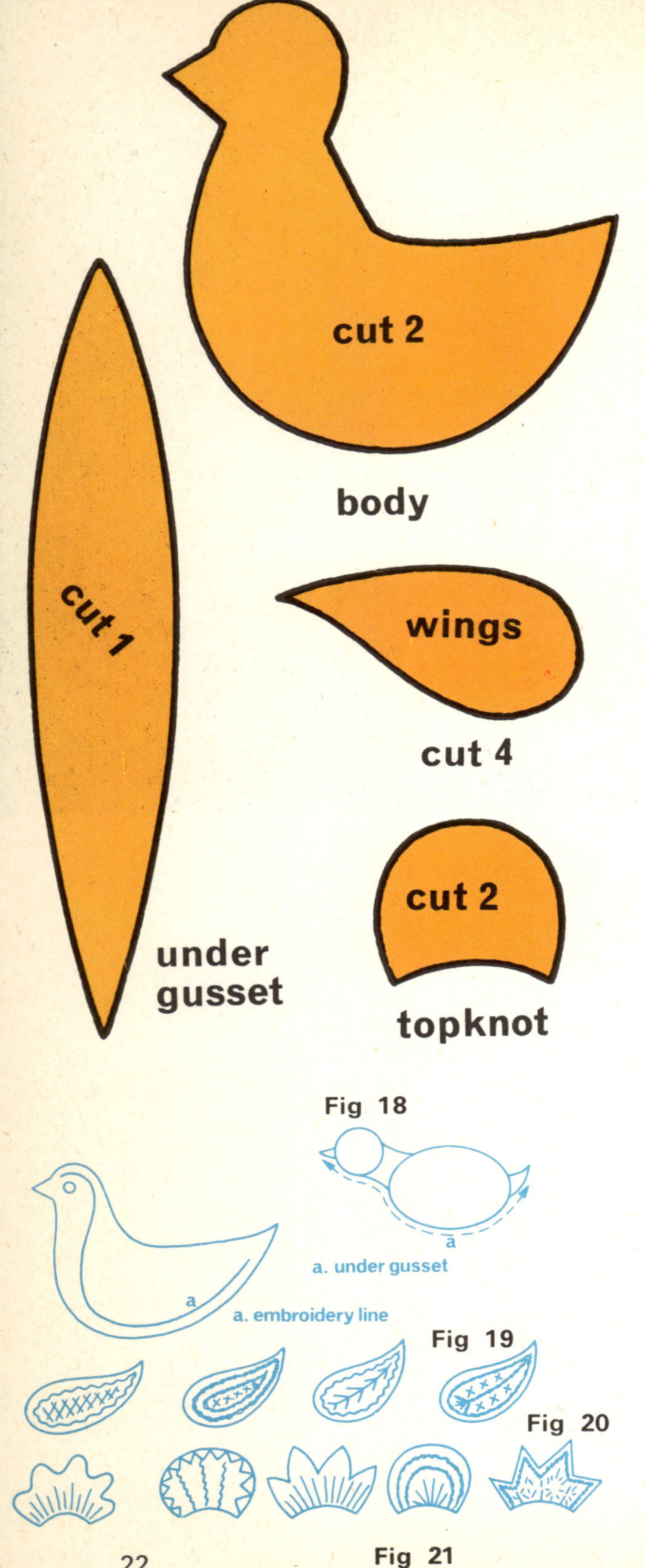

gusset, four wings, and two topknots.

Embroider all the pieces before doing any sewing up. Choose a fairly simple line design for the embroidery. Using different kinds of stitches, or variations of the same stitch, and different colours on the birds will give great variety without being too elaborate.

Mark the line of embroidery wherever possible with running stitches in contrasting cotton to avoid marking the felt. Drawing on it with a pencil will result in a wide smudgy line because of the hairy felt surface and it may be difficult to cover this with embroidery. Here, a line is used encircling the eye curves down across the neck, following the line of the body and almost reaching the tail (Fig 19). Embroider this in threaded running stitch with a row of slanting stitches in coloured fine metal-thread along the body line.

The eye is a sequin fastened down with long straight metal-thread stitches to give a starry effect.

The wings (Fig 20) have a line of fly stitch with metal-thread stitches in the spaces, surrounded with whipped running stitch. Another has a long line of double-whipped running stitch with fine metal-thread crosses above it and two lines of stem stitch on the wings following the wing shape, the inner line filled with fine metal-thread herring-bone stitch. Another one has single fly stitch in two colours worked along the body edge, and with straight metal-thread stitches on the neck and back and with a wing outlined in buttonhole stitch with a fine metal-thread cross-stitch centre. Yet another has a coloured stem stitch with a wavy metal-thread line following it and a leaf-vein design in metal-thread worked inside a stem-stitch outline on the wing.

All the topknots (Fig 21) can be different too, with a scalloped edge worked with straight stitches in metal-thread, or embroidered with metal-thread round the edge and a design in straight lines in the centre, or cut in large or small points and worked in sections in a variety of colours.

Take care to embroider all the pieces in pairs for left and right sides.

When you have completed your chosen embroidery, sew the two topknot pieces together on the right side and pin it in position on one of the side pieces. Pin the two side pieces together with right sides outside and sew them together, starting at the beak, over the head, stab stitching through the base of the topknot as well – it will not be stuffed – to the tail. Sew the gusset to one side piece, starting at the beak. Sew the gusset to the second side in easy stages, stuffing as you sew: first the head, pushing stuffing very carefully into the beak and into the seam along the topknot. Stuff firmly but not too hard. Complete the sewing up.

Sew a plain and an embroidered wing together and sew them on each side with invisible stitches.

Complete the making up of the other four birds in similar fashion.

To make the merry-go-round

Cut a circle about 12.5 cm (5″) in diameter from the card, and cut out a small segment from it (Fig 22). Lay this shape on the yellow felt and trace round it lightly with a very fine pencil point. Overlap the two cut edges of card and stick them with adhesive tape on both sides. Fit the felt shape over it, trim off any excess turnings on it and then oversew the edges on the wrong side with matching cotton.

Cut a strip of felt long enough to fit right round the outside curved edge of the felt, and 2 cm (¾″) wide.

Draw scallops (Fig 23) nearly 1.25 cm (½″) deep, round a 5p piece, and cut them out. Embroider the edge of the scallops (Fig 24) with a threaded running stitch in bright contrasting colours of embroidery silk, and sew a coloured sequin in the centre curve of each scallop. Join the two short edges and oversew the strip to the curved edge of the felt circular piece.

Cotton-reel base

Try to find a large-size cotton reel for the base because it will balance well. Cut a strip of felt long enough to go right round it and wide enough to fit from edge to edge. Cut two circles of felt to fit top and bottom. Join the side seams and sew a circle of felt to one end of it (Fig 25). Seal the hole in one end of the cotton reel with layers of adhesive tape, drop the reel, sealed end down, into the felt case, and sew on the second circle. Cut a very small cross in the top over the hole in the reel.

Make a sharp, smooth point at one end of the skewer and make a ridge about 6 mm (¼″) from the point, by binding a thick

Fig 22

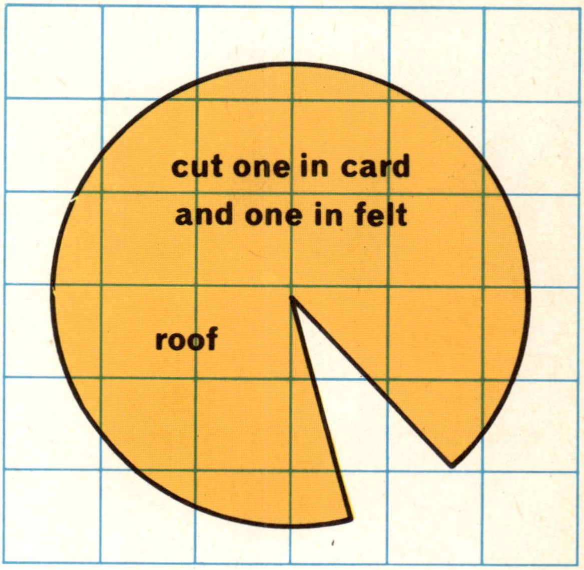

Fig 23

Fig 24

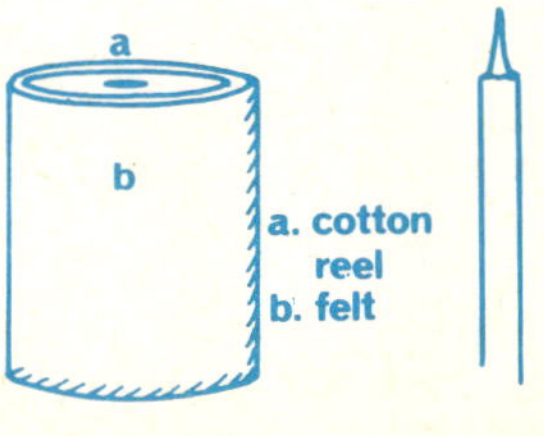

Fig 25

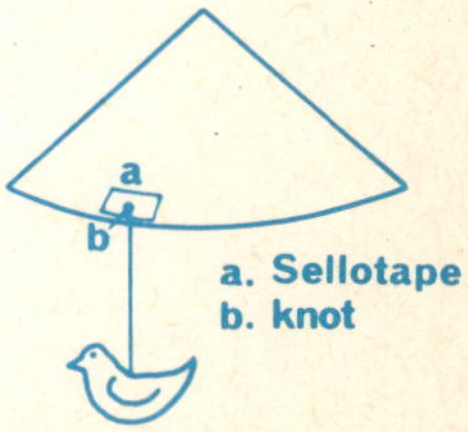

Fig 26

boat

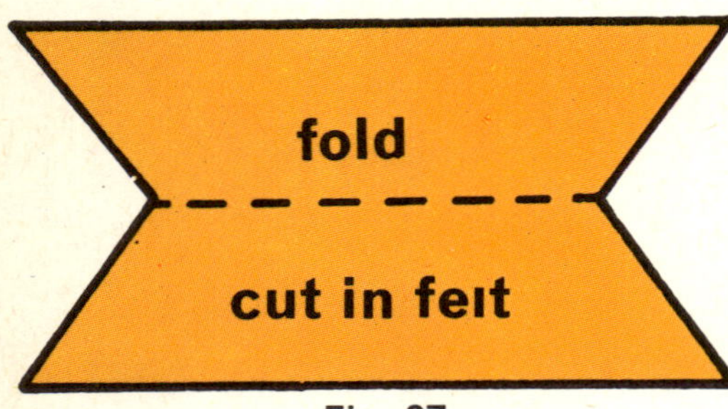

Fig 27

a

a. fold

Fig 27a

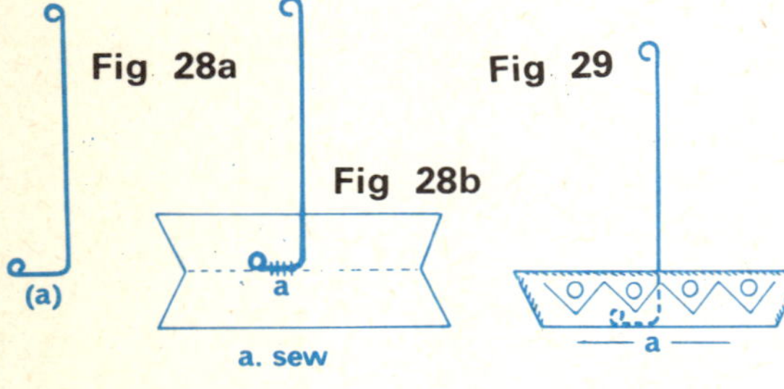

Fig 30

thread firmly all round it several times. Paint it with a thin adhesive or gum to keep it in place. Pinch round it to accentuate the ridge.

Make a small hole in the point at the top of the cone-shaped card so that the skewer point fits in and the card rests on the ridge. Mark five equidistant points round the edge of the circle and 1.25 cm to 2 cm (½" to ¾") from the edge. With nylon thread take a stitch in the birds' backs near the base of the neck and test for balance. If the head tilts forward, move the thread forward, and vice versa, until it hangs straight. Take the end of the thread through a hole at one of the marked spots, and knot it on top of the card. Seal it down with adhesive tape (Fig 26). Test the heights of the other four birds from this first one and when all are in position fit the felt canopy on top of the card one and your merry-go-round is ready.

Sailing ship mobile

This mobile of sailing ships is gay with many-coloured felts and sparkling with fine metal-thread and sequins. The sails are squares folded in half diagonally, after embroidering, and mounted on the small boats. You can use different colours for each sail and each boat, and for this quite small pieces of felt can be used.

You will need:

Small pieces of different-coloured felt; sequins; metal-threads; beads; matching cotton; a small quantity of kapok; 1.3 m (4½') of plastic-covered wire; some thin tinsel cord (the kind sold for Christmas wrappings).

Cut five squares (this is for the five ships) of felt measuring 6 cm (2¼"), five measuring 4.5 cm (1¾") and five boat shapes from the template shown here. The boat will be folded along the dotted line which is the base (Fig 27).

Cut five pieces of wire 10 cm (4¼") long for the masts. Twist each end of wire into a small ring and bend nearly 1.25 cm (½") at right angles at one end of each (Fig 28a).

Embroider each boat each side of the base line, in a very simple design.

Place a mast with the short side 'a' along the base of the boat so that the 'mast' is in the centre, and sew it in place (Fig 28b).

Fold the boat in half with the right sides outside and sew from the base, up one side and along the top as far as the mast. Stuff this half very lightly with small pieces of kapok, keeping it smooth. Continue sewing and stuffing along the top. Sew up the side. Mark the diagonal line on a square with running stitches and embroider a motif on each side of the line (Fig 29). The designs used are shown in Fig 30. They combine the use of sequins with various coloured fine metal-thread.

Fold each square along the diagonal with right sides outside, and oversew the edges (Fig 31). Attach it to the mast at top and bottom with a few stitches taken round the wire, and also catch it down to the end of the boat. Put one large and one smaller sail on each boat (Fig 32).

Cut five small pennants, embroider and sew one on each masthead.

To make the mobile frame

Cut three pieces of wire, one piece 35.5 cm (14") long and two pieces 21 cm (8½") long. The two short wires will be suspended from each end of the long wire. Cut about 50 cm (20") length of tinsel cord and split it, using a single strand. Make a small notch with a nail file in the middle of the long wire and tie the cord round it so that there is a short length to tie on the boat and a longer piece for suspending the mobile. Use a clove hitch knot for this (Fig 33). Tie shorter lengths of cord like this to the middles of the other two wires.

Bend each end of each wire into a small loop. Tie a small loop in the short cord on the long wire, about 2.5 cm (1") from the wire and slip it over the wire loop in the ship's mast. Cut two lengths of cord about 30 cm (12") long, split them and make a loop in one end of each piece. Slip them over the wire loops in the other ships' masts (Fig 34). Lay out the wires in hanging position and decide on the position for each ship. To be really effective they should hang at different levels. Tie small loops in the cord at the required level and slip over the wire loops on the frame. A last loop tied in the hanging cord and the mobile is ready. The ships should be able to swing freely without touching one another.

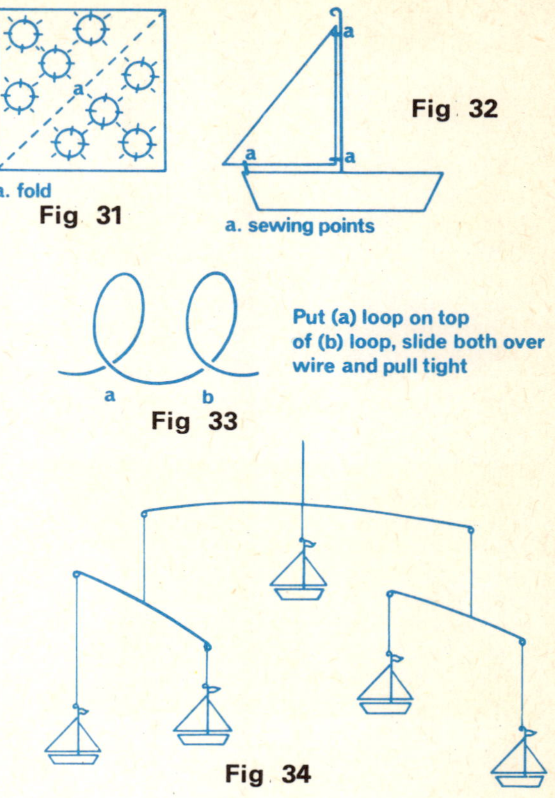

Fig 31

Fig 32

Fig 33

Fig 34

A royal elephant

A royal elephant, richly decorated and embroidered, carries his prince on his back in a howdah, with a young attendant mahout to guide him. He stands nearly 22.8 cm (9'') tall and is made of grey felt, which shows up his gay colouring. Over his back, under the howdah, is an embroidered brocade saddle cloth.

You will need:

A piece of grey felt 51 cm (20'') square; a small piece of black felt for the soles of the feet and for his eyes; some white felt for his tusks; a length of wire for the tusks, trunk and legs; a piece of brocade 20 cm by 15 cm (8'' by 6''); some fringe; kapok or similar for stuffing; beads; sequins; embroidery silks; grey cotton.

The template is cut from a silhouette including the trunk (Fig 35). The under gusset for the legs to make him stand up is cut from the same silhouette of the legs, from a curved line following the under-body shape and stretching from near the end of the inner trunk at the mouth, to the tail (Fig 36).

The back gusset stretches from a point near the end of the trunk, over the head and back, to the tail. It is pointed at each end, is narrow at the trunk, broadening very gradually to its widest part at the top of the head and near the shoulders.

Draw round the templates on to the grey felt, reversing the template when drawing each second piece.

Cut two body pieces, two under gussets, one back gusset, and four ear pieces from the grey felt; four oval soles and two small eye circles from the black felt; and four strips in white felt, pointed at one end for the tusks.

Embroider the legs of the body pieces, the sides of the trunk, and two of the ear pieces, pairing them all for left and right sides. Sew the black felt eyes in position near the top of the head and embroider a circle round them; add sequins and beads to the coloured embroidery for a rich effect.

Sew in the back gusset, matching the joining points on the two body pieces. Oversew the curved seam of the under gusset on the wrong side. Pin it on to one of the body pieces, starting at the front edge of the foot, up the leg and down the trunk. Sew this piece, sewing from the trunk and down the front seam of the front leg. Fasten off here.

Sew up a couple of centimetres of the back seam of the front leg, and leave the thread hanging while you sew a sole piece to the leg, the long side of the oval stretching from the front seam to the back seam. Oversew the edges.

Cut a piece of wire 35.5 cm (14'') long and mark the centre of it. Twist each end into a small, flat loop and bend them at right angles to the main wire. Pad the loop with a little stuffing. Place the wire loop flat on the sole and pad all round loop and wire, keeping the wire in the middle of the leg. Sew the back seam a little at a time, and stuff firmly, completely enclosing the wire (Fig 37).

Sew the under body and down the front seam of the back leg. Fasten off at the foot. Sew the back leg in the same way as the front leg, inserting a second length of wire and sewing and stuffing the leg a little at a time. Sew the seam round the end of the trunk between the ends of the two gussets.

Cut a piece of wire about 23 cm (9'') long, and twist one end up to cover the sharp end of the wire. Pad with a little kapok and push the end into the trunk, padding all round it with small pieces of stuffing, keeping it firm but not hard. Twist the other end of the wire round the marked centre of the front-leg wire.

Pin the under gusset to the second body piece, starting again from the front foot to the trunk and carefully matching the pinning with the side already sewn. Start sewing from the trunk, a little at a time, and padding as you sew, all round the trunk wire, keeping it away from the edges. Stuff the head firmly and smoothly, keeping it a good shape.

Continue sewing down the front seam of the front leg, fastening off at the foot. Pad the loop of the other end of the front leg wire and finish off in the same way, fastening off at the top of the leg.

Stuff the front part of the body, packing stuffing firmly round all the wires, particularly at the tops of the legs. Finish off the back leg in the same way as the others, leaving the under body seam, between the legs, open for stuffing. Complete the stuffing and sew up the opening.

Make a short cord in black wool, fringe the ends and sew on for a tail.

body
cut 2
back
gusset
cut 1
under gusset
cut 2
ear
cut 4
a. back
b. front
c. side
a
b
c
sole
cut 4
eye
cut 2
sewing line
tusk
cut 4
Fig 35

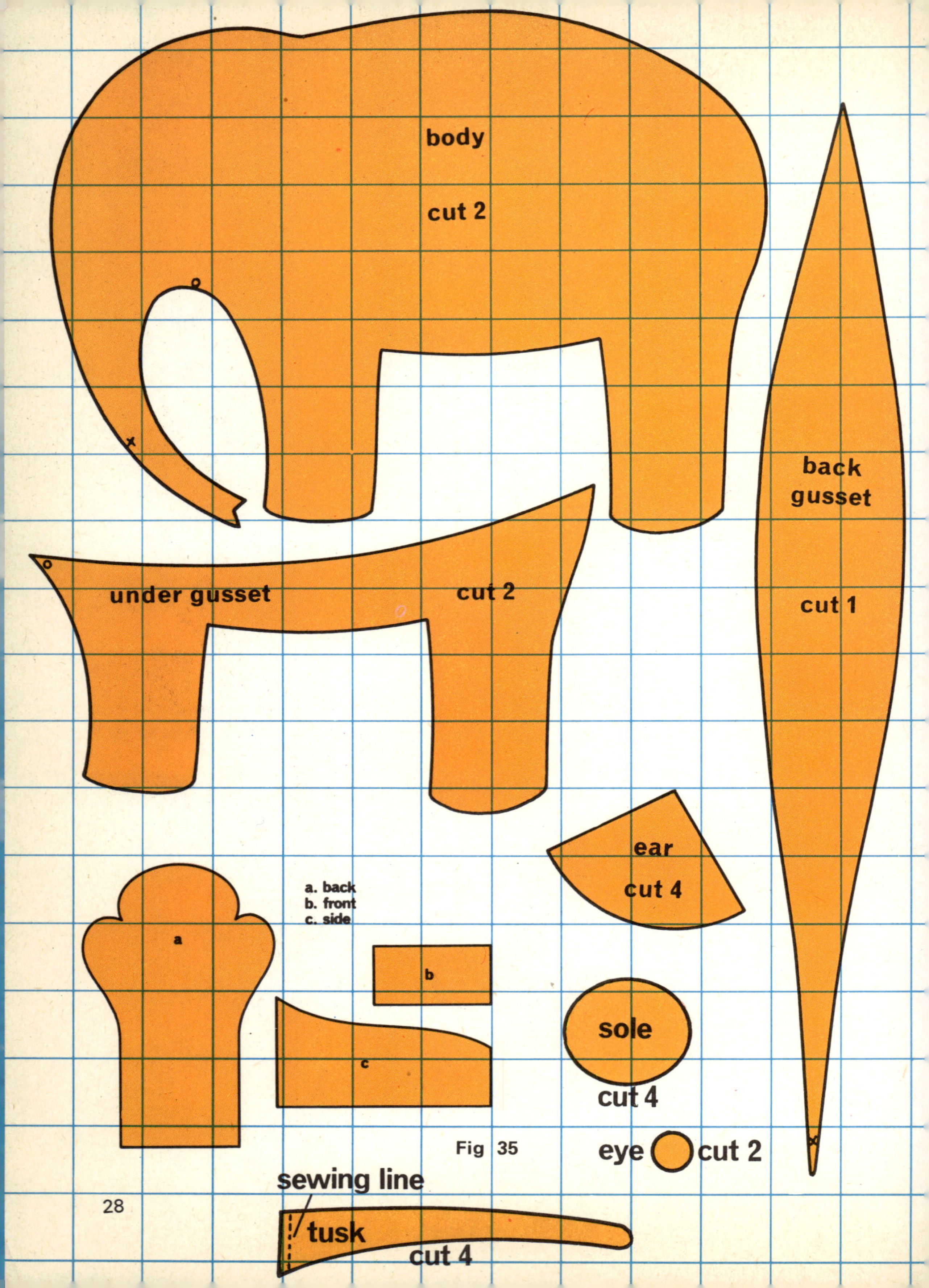

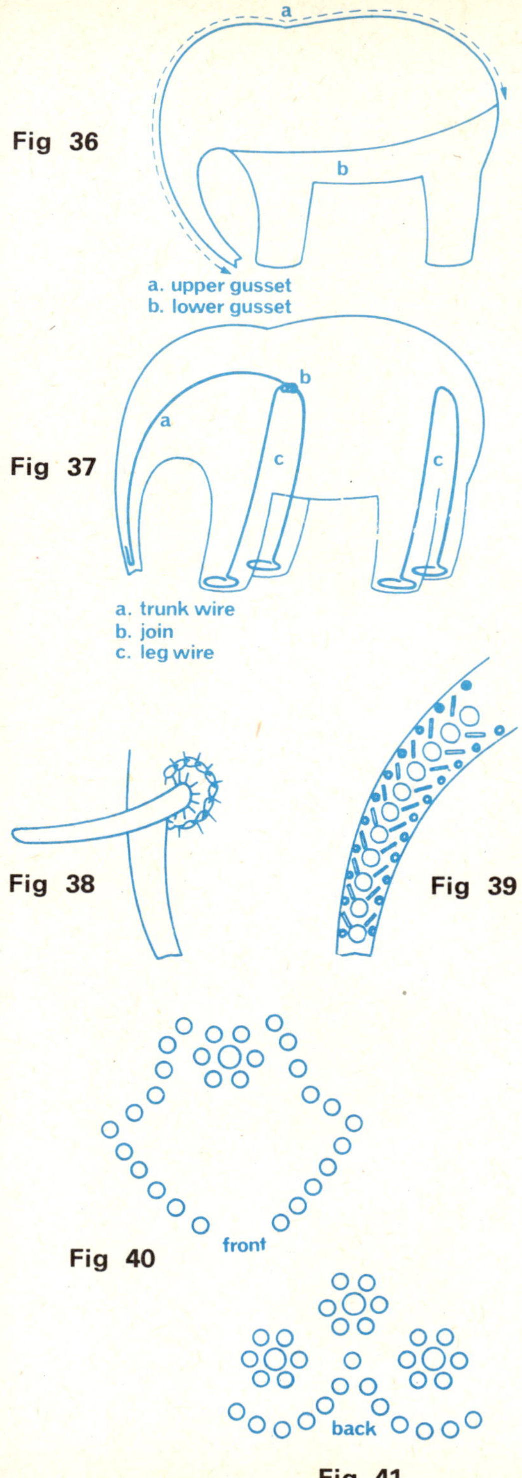

Fig 36

Fig 37

Fig 38

Fig 39

Fig 40

Fig 41

Join together two pieces for each ear, one embroidered and one plain, pairing them for left and right sides. Sew in place just behind the eyes, pointing to the back.

For the tusks, cut two pieces of wire 5 cm (2″) longer than the felt. Join two pieces of the felt along one seam and about 1.25 cm (½″) along the second seam. Turn back one end of the wire, pad it thinly with kapok, or a strip of thin material, and insert in the tusk, pushing it gently down to the point. Continue sewing the seam, pushing in kapok round the wire as you sew. About 3 cm (1¾″) of wire should be left at the end of the tusk. Make a very small hole beside the top of the trunk and push in the bare wire. Sew the open end of the tusk on to the body, and work a ring of embroidery around the join (Fig 38). Make up the second tusk in the same way.

Sew a line of bright red sequins down the front of the trunk with bugle beads and small beads in between them and along the side (Fig 39). Couch down a thick bright silk thread over the joins of trunk and gusset.

Make a narrow hem on each of the edges of brocade, decorate the long sides with embroidery and sequins and sew fringe along the short sides. Sew it in place on the back.

The howdah

This is made from four shaped pieces of thick card, each covered with embroidered felt and then joined together to form a hollow box. The back is high and throne-like, the sides curving down to a narrow front (Fig 35).

In thick card, cut one back, two sides and one front piece. Trace round the card shapes on to the felt, cutting two backs, two fronts and four sides, all slightly larger than the card to allow for its thickness.

Embroider both pieces for the back, one piece for the front and one for each side, left and right (Figs 40 and 41).

Join the two back pieces together with right sides outside; halfway to the top of the back curve insert the card shape and continue sewing, enclosing the card. Join three sides of the front pieces, insert the card and sew the fourth side. Join the curved edges and the short side of the side pieces, insert the cards and sew up the remaining side. Join all the pieces together with right sides outside.

Sew the howdah in place on the

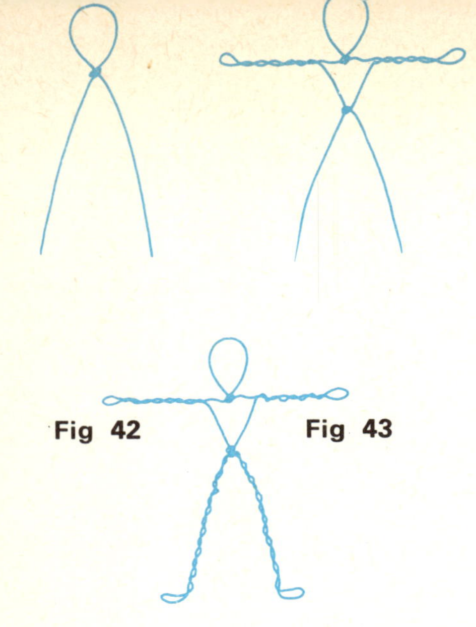

Fig 42

Fig 43

Fig 44

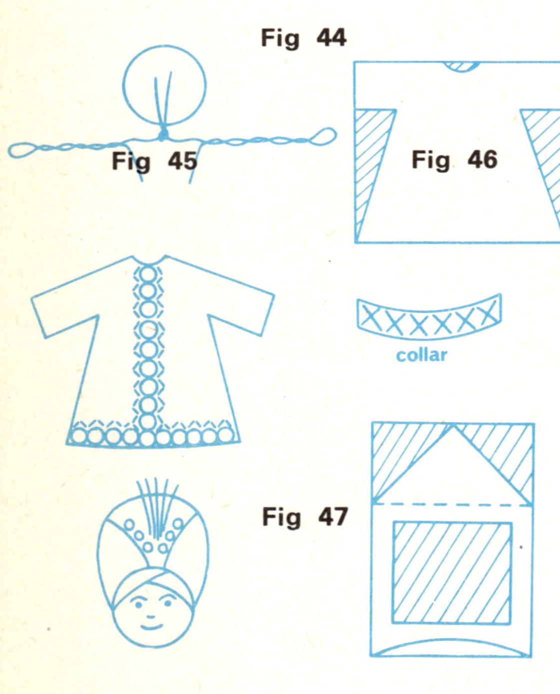

Fig 45

Fig 46

Fig 47

Fig 48

Fig 49

elephant's back on top of the brocade, taking stitches through the actual back if possible to keep it firmly in place.

The little prince

He is made from soft wire covered with strips of dark nylon stocking; his head is a polystyrene ball or could be a loop of wire padded. He is nearly 15 cm (6'') tall.

You will need:

A piece of wire about 76 cm (30'') long; a 2.5 cm (1'') polystyrene ball; some dark nylon stocking; some pieces of gay silks to dress him; some sequins and beads.

Make the frame for his body from the piece of wire. Fold it in half, insert one finger in the fold and twist, making a small loop (Fig 42). Bend back each wire about 6 cm (2½'') from the twist, and twist these wires together for the arms, leaving a small loop at each end for the hands (Fig 43). Bring the two ends of wire together and twist together at the waist forming a triangle for the body. Bend back the remaining ends of wire and twist round the waist, forming two large loops; then twist these into legs, leaving small loops for the feet (Fig 44).

Twist a strip of bias cut material round the limbs and body and cover all with strips of dark-coloured nylon.

Cut the loop of wire at the head to make two ends. Make a small hole in the polystyrene ball and push in the two ends firmly (Fig 45). Cover the ball with the dark nylon, keeping the front smooth and free from wrinkles for the face. Draw the features with a felt-tip pen.

Trousers

Make his full trousers, gathered round the ankles, in bright blue metal-thread material, two rectangles 7.5 cm by 6 cm (3'' by 2½'').

Fold each piece in half lengthways and seam them together for half the length for the legs, then join both legs together with a back and front seam. Make a small turning at the legs and gather them to fit closely round the ankles. The waist is likewise gathered up and sewn to the figure.

Tunic

Over these he wears a tunic top in white satin, cut from a rectangle 12.5 cm by 9 cm

(5″ by 3½″). Fold it in half and cut out the sides (Fig 46).

Sew the side and arm seams. Turn under small hems at sleeves, neck and bottom and sew the front and bottom edge closely with red and blue sequins and fine metal-thread crosses in green and gold (Fig 47). A neckband embroidered with fine metal-thread crosses encircles the neck closely.

A turban in material matching the trousers is folded round the head, envelope fashion, the folds coming in the front and fastened with red sequins with a plume of fine gold metal-thread (Fig 48). He will sit proudly in the howdah.

His elephant's mahout

You will need:

About twelve black pipe cleaners and some scraps of white cambric for his turban and loincloth.

Fold a pipe cleaner in half, forming a small loop as foundation for the head. Twist two more for the arms, leaving very small loops for the hands. Twist together the ends of head and arms. Twist on to them two more pipe cleaners for the body and two more for each leg, to the bottom of the body, and twist all the ends firmly. Bind two more cleaners round the top of the body to give it some shape – it will be bare – and bind some round the head loop to shape the head. Do not make the head too large.

Cut a crossway strip of cambric and bind it round the head in three or four folds for a turban, and sew the end at the back. Cut a second, wider crossway strip and fold it round legs and waist for a loincloth, sewing the ends underneath out of sight.

Bend the legs outward and down to make knees and you will find that he sits quite well on the elephant's neck, above the ears. A pipe cleaner sewn on one hand could be his goad.

Another howdah

A different type of howdah with closed sides and roof can also be made from thick card covered with felt.

You will need:

Four rectangles of card measuring 6 cm by 10 cm (2½″ by 4″) (the 10 cm (4″) to be the height).

Cut out all the shaded parts (Fig 49) and score across the dotted line for the roof. The two end pieces will need a slight curve cut out from the bottom to enable the howdah to fit over the elephant's back.

Trace round the cut-out card shape on to some coloured felt and cut out eight shapes, remembering to cut them slightly larger than the cards.

Embroider four of the pieces with sequins and fine metal-thread and sew together an embroidered piece and a plain piece, sewing round three edges and leaving the roof open.

Score the dotted line on the card and bend the roof triangle away from the cut. This scored side will be the outside so that it bends in towards the centre.

Insert a card and complete the oversewing of the roof and the window.

Repeat this for the other three sides and then sew them all together, first the sides and then the roof. Sew it on to the elephant's back like the other.

A decorated camel

He is a fine fellow and obviously knows he is a very superior animal. Gaily decorated, he is made in purple felt, has a silky mane and tail laced with silver. His coat sparkles with fine metal-thread and sequins and he has a very splendid saddle cloth for his master or mistress to sit on.

You will need:

A piece of purple felt 40 cm by 61 cm (16″ by 24″); some soft, white, nylon, silky wool; a 10 cm (4″) square of bright pink felt for a saddle cloth; embroidery silks; fine metal-thread; coloured sequins; beads; silver cord; little pearls or gold beads; kapok or similar for stuffing; purple cotton.

The under gusset is curved to follow the line of his curved chest and stretches up to reach just under his chin and then round to his tail, following the curve of the under body (Fig 52).

Trace round the templates on to the felt with a very sharp white pencil, and cut out two body pieces, two under gussets, one back gusset, two ears, and four soles in purple felt.

Trace each side of the camel on to thin

tracing or tissue paper and draw the embroidery design. Pin the paper on to the felt body piece and sew the design through the paper and felt with tiny running stitches in cotton. When finished, tear away the paper and embroider on top of the running stitches. It is a branching design from a central stem on each leg (Fig 50). The one on

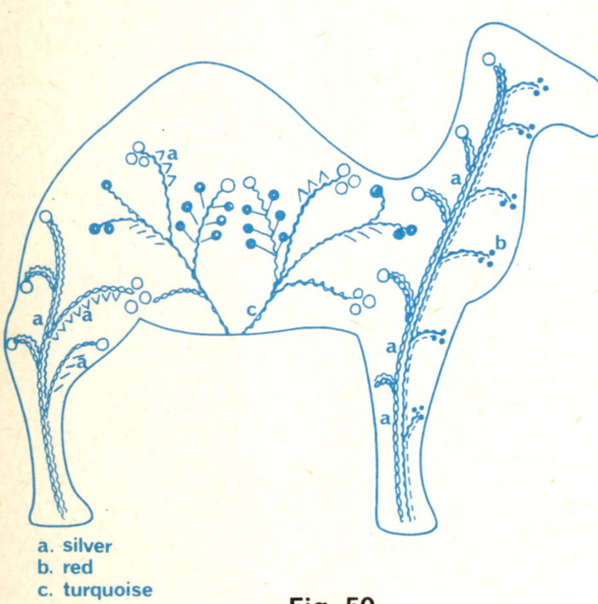

Fig 50

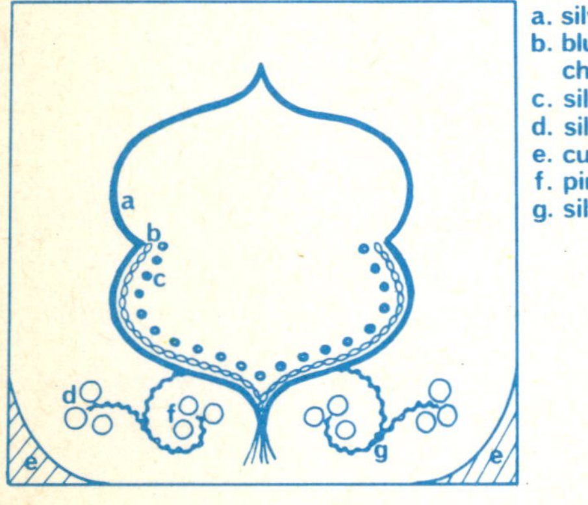

Fig 51

the front leg starts near the foot and stretches to the face with little branches decorated with beads and sequins on each side. It is worked in threaded and whipped running stitch with fine silver metal-thread chain stitch on one side of it. That on the hind leg is similar but shorter. In between them, on the broad space of body near the hump, it is more intricate, but following the same style and using the same stitches. Embroider both sides, pairing them for left and right.

For an eye, embroider a crescent in fine silver metal-thread in chain stitch with straight stitches radiating from it for eye lashes.

Sew the back gusset to the two body pieces. Join the two under gussets, oversewing the curved seam on the wrong side. Pin it to one of the body pieces, with right sides outside. Sew, starting from the neck, down the front seam of the front leg and fasten off. Leave the base of the foot unsewn. Sew for 2.5 cm (1″) along the inner seam of the leg. Leave the thread hanging, and sew a sole piece on to the foot, the length of it stretching from back to front between the two seams.

Stuff this foot very carefully and very firmly with small pieces of stuffing. Carry on sewing and stuffing, sewing a little at a time. Repeat this for the back leg.

Make a short cord for a tail with long, fringed ends. Interweave the cord with fine silver metal-thread and bind the fringed end with silver. Tie a knot in the other end and pin it in place under the point of the upper gusset.

Sew up the seam under the chin and down to the beginning of the under gusset. Stuff the head softly but firmly, pushing stuffing well into the muzzle and the seams to keep a good shape.

Pin the second body piece to the under gusset, starting at the neck. Follow the directions for sewing the front leg. Now stuff the neck, pushing the stuffing well up into the head, making sure it is smooth and has no weak places. Leave the under-body seam open. Sew the inner seam of the back leg and fasten off. Sew up 2.5 cm (1″) of the outer seam and then sew on the sole. Stuff the foot. Continue sewing and stuffing about 2.5 cm (1″) at a time. Sew up the remainder of the seam, sewing in the tail as well. Stuff the rest of the body and sew up the under seam.

Fold the corners of the straight edges of

the ears to the centre, and sew in place on the head near the top and pointing backwards.

Embroider nostrils with a single chain stitch and a mouth curve in chain stitch in black embroidery silk.

Sew loops of the white nylon wool across the chest from under the chin to just under the bulge in the chest. Cut the loops and fluff out the wool.

Embroider a scallop-edged design (Fig 51) on the pink felt square. Draw the design on thin paper and transfer it to the felt in the same way as for the camel. Embroider it with a row of silver cord couched down following the shape; inside this, a row of fine blue metal-thread chain stitch and inside this a row of silver beads. The design is completed by two scrolls each side of the point in fine silver metal-thread chain stitch with three sequins sewn at each scroll end.

Sew the saddle cloth in place on the hump with invisible stitches.

Sew a small string of tiny seed pearls or gold beads as a diadem on the head with a pearl drop on the forehead.

A silver cord bridle completes your camel.

An Italian flower donkey

This little grey donkey is walking, not just standing as the other toy animals have been.

To make him you will need:

Grey felt; a small piece of orange felt for a hat; some red felt for the panniers; some embroidery silks; sequins; beads; fine metal-thread; black wool for a tail; kapok for stuffing; some grey cotton.

As the donkey is walking you will have to make a more complicated template, because the two sides are different and so are the two under-gusset pieces. If you are drawing your own silhouette to make templates, you must draw a right and a left side, with the front and back legs in the correct position for walking (Fig 53).

Make a template for each side. Draw a curved line on each of them from chest to tail, and each side will then have its own under gusset. Check that the under gusset curves stretch between identical points on both chests and tails. The head and back gusset are in one, stretching from under the nose, over the head and back, to the tail. The ears are large and leaf-shaped.

Cut two sides, two under and one top gusset, two ears.

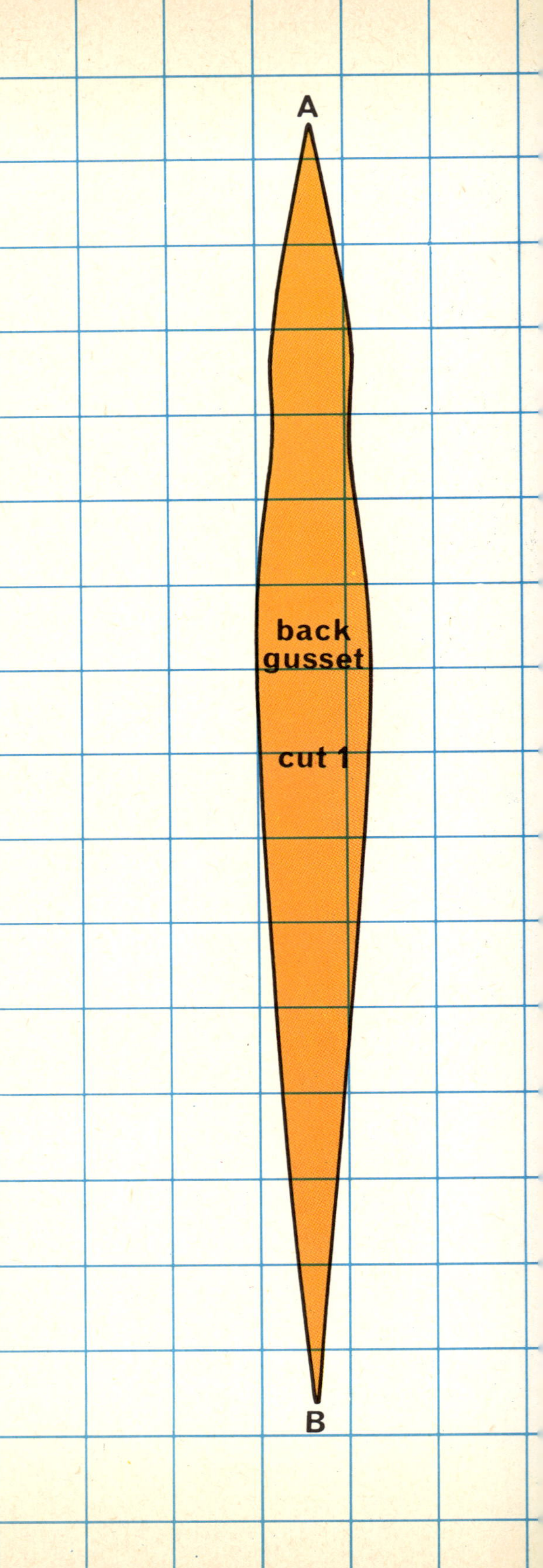

A
B
X
body
cut 2
Y
ear
cut 2
decoration
pattern
for
saddle
cloth
X
Y
under gusset
cut 2
sole
cut 4

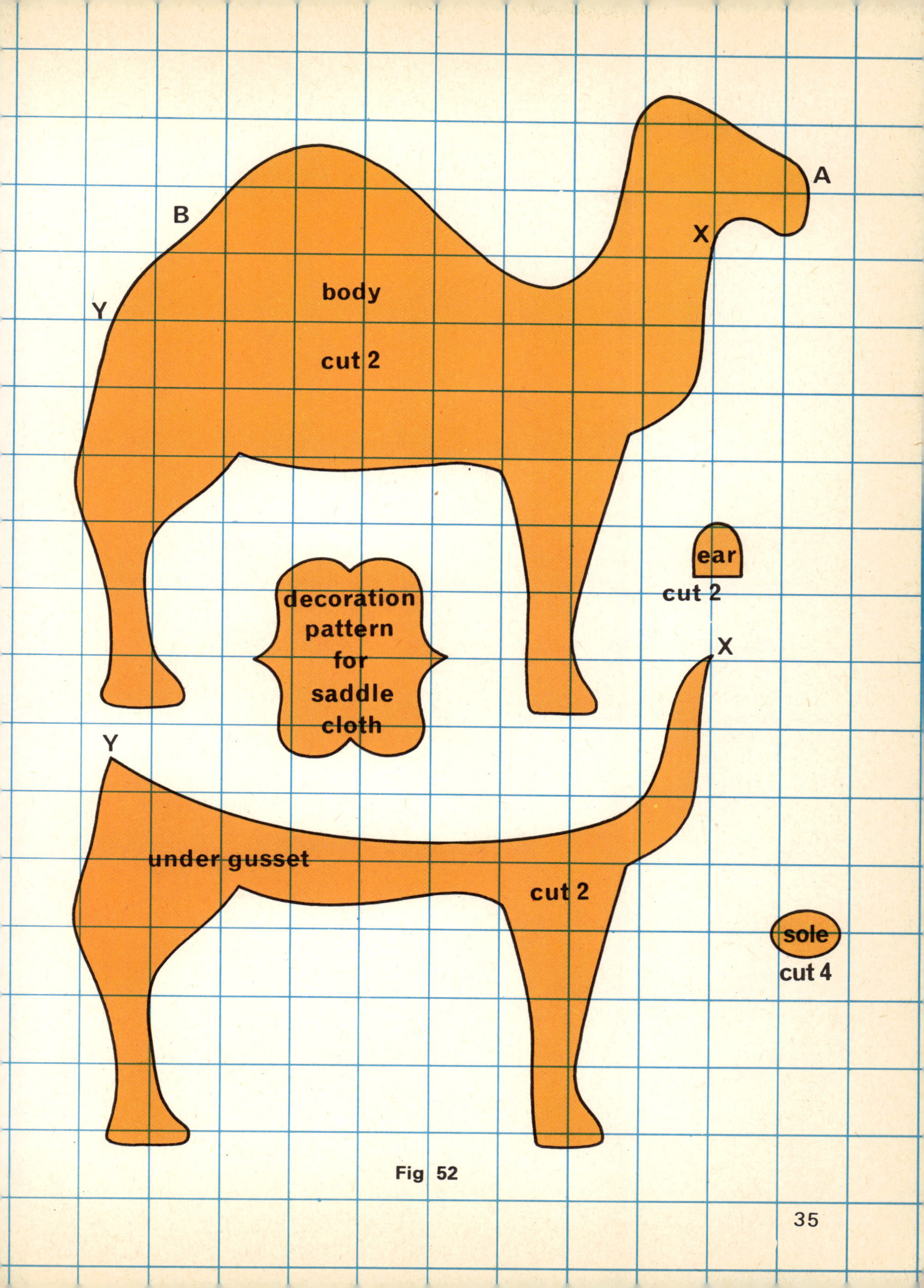

Fig 52

left side
cut 1
A
B
donkey hat
cut 1
B
ear
cut
2
back
gusset
cut 1
right side
cut 1
A
B
cut 2
pannier base
pannier top
cut 2
A
pannier
centre front
cut 2
right under gusset cut 1
left under gusset cut 1
Fig 53

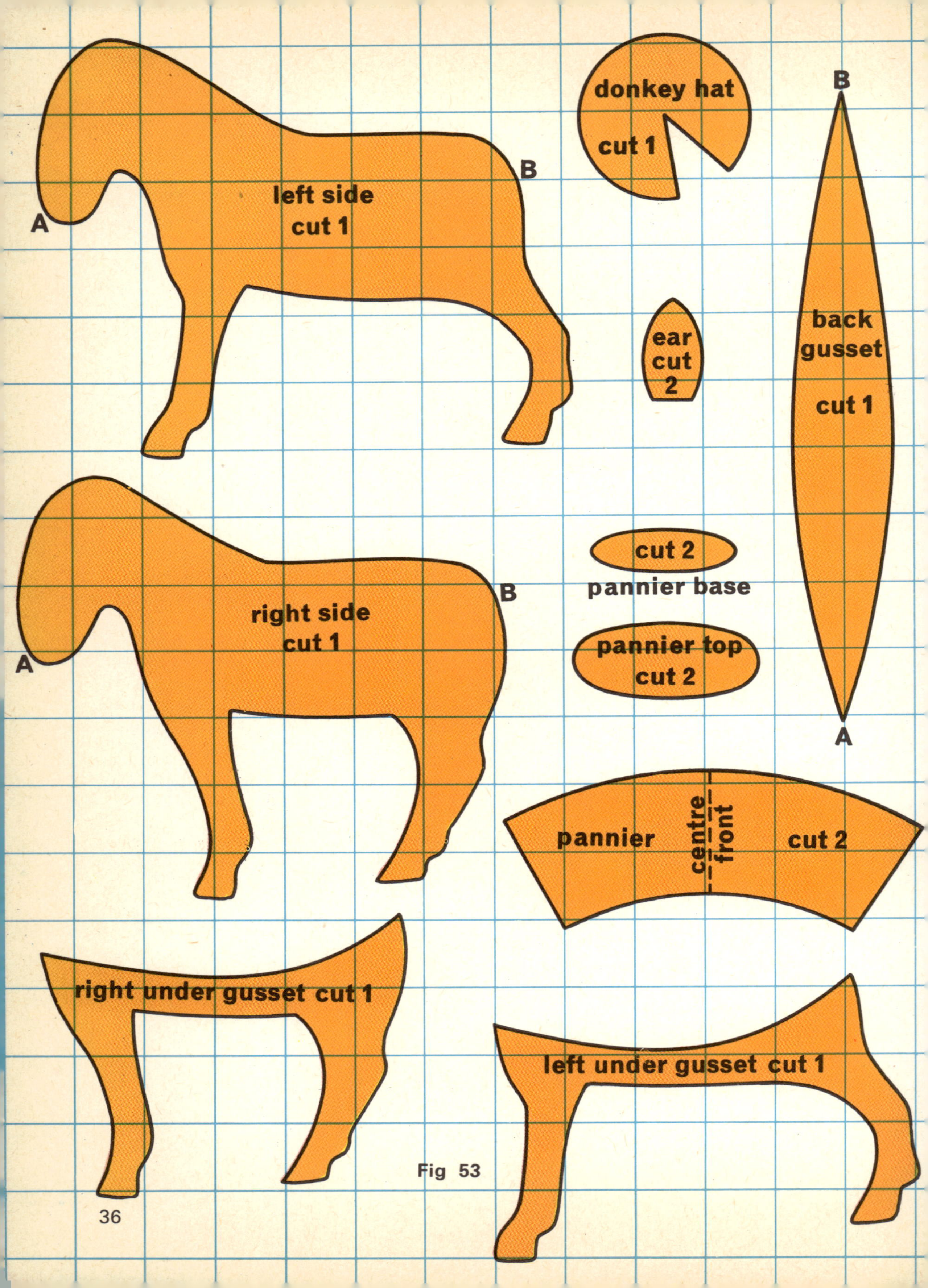

Join the two sides to the head gusset on the right side, starting each time from the nose (A) and matching the finishing point at the neck (B).

Join the curved sides of the under gussets on the wrong side, and sew one body side piece on to it, starting from the neck. Sew down the front seam of the front leg, along the sole, and about 2.5 cm (1") of the back seam. Now stuff the foot very firmly with small pieces of kapok. Finish the leg seam and stuff the rest of the leg. Continue along the under body and sew the back leg in similar manner as the front leg.

Pin the grey wool tail in position at the top of the gusset.

Sew the back seam from the nose to the top of the neck, and stuff the head, pushing stuffing carefully into the seams and keeping the head a good shape.

Pin the under gusset to the second side, matching pinning points at the feet and the tops of the legs.

Sew and stuff the front leg, and then the back leg, leaving the middle of the body seam open for stuffing. Fill the rest of the body, pushing the stuffing well into the tops of the legs to keep them firm. Sew the tail in with the final seam.

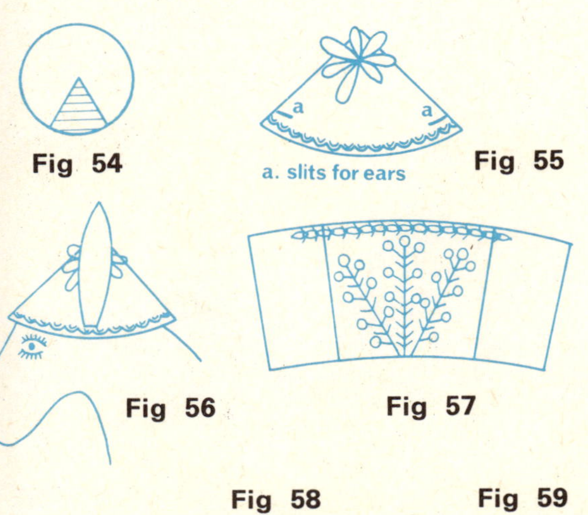

Fig 54

Fig 55

Fig 56

Fig 57

Fig 58

Fig 59

Hat

For the hat, cut a circle of felt on a 7.6 cm (3") diameter, and cut out a segment of it, leaving about 2 cm (¾") of the circle (Fig 54). Join the two straight sides to make a shallow cone. Embroider the edge with loops of coloured silks. Mark the two places for the ears on the head and cut two small slits in the hat to correspond with these (Fig 55). Push the bottoms of the ears into the slits and sew them in place. Sew the ears to the head, keeping them upright (Fig 56). Sew the hat on to the head with invisible stitches.

Cut two panniers from the template and two tops and two bases.

Embroider the middle section of each pannier—this will be its front. At the top overlay a line of orange chain stitch with fine silver metal-thread fly stitch (Fig 57). Sew three lines of green fly stitch spraying out from the bottom edge. Sew blue and silver sequins down each side of the fly stitch. Join the two straight edges and sew the base piece on to the bottom edge of the pannier.

Pack some kapok into the pannier.

Thread two strands of purple silk into a large-eyed needle and sew loops all over the oval for the top of the pannier (Fig 58). Sew scattered loops of yellow among them and finish with loops of fine green metal-thread between them. Cut the metal-thread loops. Sew this oval on to the top of the pannier enclosing the stuffing.

Cut a rectangle of orange felt 10 cm by 5 cm (4" by 2") to fit over the donkey's back.

Embroider the centre parts of the two long sides with fine silver metal-thread herring-bone stitch.

Sew the panniers on each side, fit it on to the donkey's back and fasten it in place with a band of felt sewn underneath the body.

Embroider two almond-shaped eyes in black stem stitch with straight stitches above for lashes and an orange centre.

Tie a cotton round the neck as a guide and embroider a wreath of flowers with sequin centres and red bead petals and fine green metal-thread leaves round the neck (Fig 59).

An open chain stitch each side of the nose for nostrils and a curved line of stem stitch for a mouth completes the little donkey.

CHAPTER TWO

All kinds of dolls

It is a very interesting hobby to make a collection of dolls from different kinds of materials and then to dress them in the national costume of different countries.

Because felt does not fray, it needs no turnings; but if you make your doll in fabric, then you must allow 1.25 cm (½") extra for turnings.

Dolls from felt

These dolls are easy to make because felt is so easy to work with. It is soft and presents no difficulty in cutting or sewing, and does not fray when it is cut, so that no turnings are needed in its making up.

Felt is easy for children to use for dressing their dolls too—its colours are gay and very varied and when the dolls are small, like peg dolls, it is the most successful means of dressing them.

Things to remember

Be careful when pinning felt because pale colours do mark easily, and always pin as near to the edge as possible so that any marks will be hidden by the sewing.

When leaving unfinished work, always stick the needle in on the edge or in some stitching or embroidery already done.

When transferring designs for embroidering to felt, trace the design on to thin paper, place this in position for the embroidery and work running stitch in contrasting cotton through paper and felt, afterwards tearing away the paper. The stitching or embroidery will hide the running stitches, if they cannot be pulled out.

When tracing round templates, as for instance, for a doll, use a sharply pointed pencil and do not press down too heavily. You may find that the resulting outline is a smudgy thick line, so always trace on the wrong side of the material, and cut out the shape, if possible, inside the traced lines; otherwise seams may appear grubby and soiled.

Most of the dolls are sewn together on the right side, either with oversewing or stab stitch, which in appearance is rather like running stitch. Running stitch itself should not be used because when putting the needle in and out in one motion, the thickness of the felt will tend to stretch one side more than the other, resulting in a puckered finish. Stab stitch is sewn by inserting the needle at right angles from front to back, and then at right angles again from back to front. In this way, both edges of material are kept together, one not moving more than the other.

The simple doll

The template of it is all in one with arms and legs (Fig 1).

You will need:

Felt; some soft stuffing material like kapok; embroidery silks; wool or silk for making hair; material for dressing.

There are two ways of sewing up felt dolls, either by oversewing or by stab stitch. If you are going to oversew, then trace round the template twice and cut out the pieces, cutting just inside the pencil lines.

Pin the two pieces together, matching the heads, hands and feet, and then oversew, starting from the top of a leg, round the legs, arms and head, leaving one side open for stuffing.

If using stab stitch, fold the felt in half and trace one outline on to the doubled material. Tack round the outside of the shape (Fig 2),

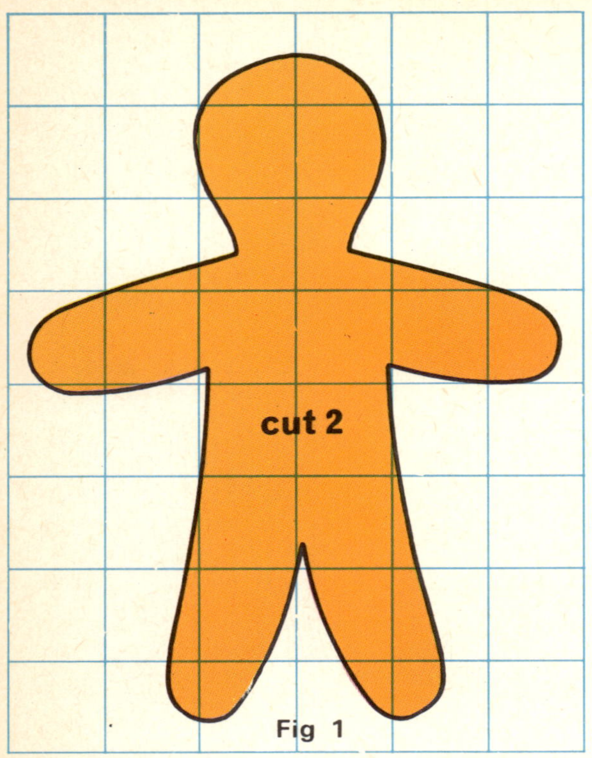

Fig 1

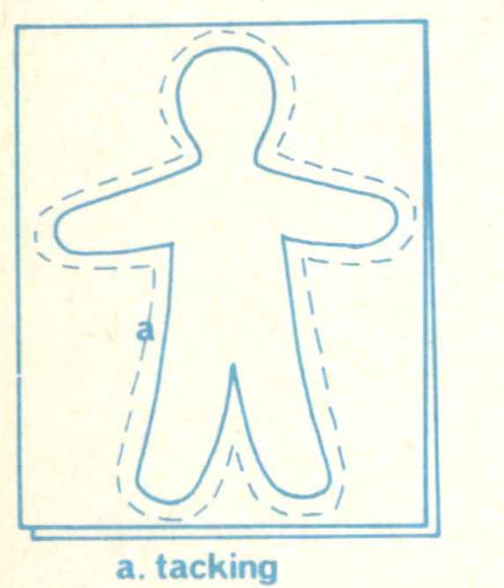

Fig 2

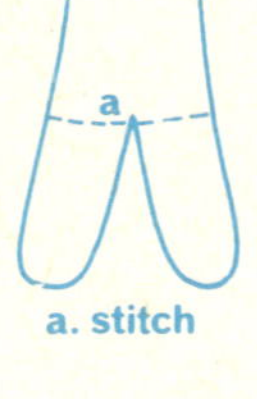

Fig 3

Fig 4 Fig 5

and stab stitch it together, leaving one side open for stuffing. When finished, trim off the surplus felt as close as possible to the stitching.

Legs

Stuff the legs first, pushing the stuffing gently into the feet with a blunted pencil or orange stick. Stuff thinly near the tops of the legs if you are going to make a jointed leg so that the doll can sit. To do this, sew a row of close stab stitch or back stitch across the tops of the legs (Fig 3).

Head and arms

Stuff the head and arms, keeping the parts flat rather than round, or the stitches may pull. Take care, too, not to pull too hard on the corners of the opening or the felt may tear. Stuff the rest of the body and sew up the opening.

Features

Embroider the features with embroidery silks; felt-tip pens are not very successful on felt, because the hairy surface makes the outline smudgy.

Hair

Hair can be made in several ways—for straight hair, or plaits, cut lengths of wool to reach from shoulder to shoulder over the head (Fig 4). Spread them out over the back of the head and catch them down the centre with back stitch, like a parting. Bunch them together at the side and tie with bows, or plait the ends. Curls can be made by threading a darning needle with brown or yellow wool; take a stitch through the head on a previously marked hair line across the forehead, place a finger on the strand of wool close to the head and wind it two or three times round the finger. Slip the loops off and catch them down on the head with a couple of stitches through all the loops. Repeat this, sewing the loops close together all along the hairline, then filling in the rest of the head (Fig 5). Separate the loops by ruffling them with your hand.

Dress

Make a little Spanish bib dress from a piece of material 10 cm by 25 cm (4″ by 10″) using the directions for it on p 48.

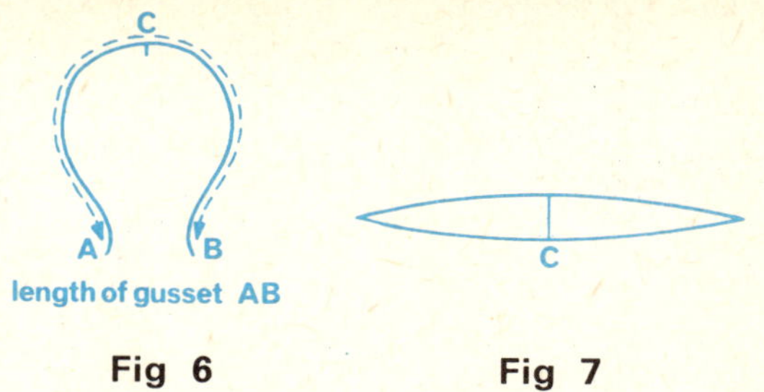

Fig 6 Fig 7

Small doll with head gusset

The pattern for the simple doll can be used for a little doll which has a much rounder head, by adding a gusset, from the neck one side to the other, and using oversewing to make it up.

Measure the length from the neck, over the head to the neck at the other side, and cut a gusset this length, pointed at each end and 1.25 cm (½") wide at the widest part at the top of the head (Figs 6 and 7).

Pin the gusset in place on one piece and oversew it in place. Pin the second side, matching points with the first side and oversew it. Make up the rest of the little doll as before, leaving an opening for stuffing and finishing it off in the same way.

Features

Features for it can be made from two small circles in blue felt, sewn on with straight stitches for eyelashes, and a small crescent shape for a smiling mouth.

Hair

Hair can be made in a fringe of felt. Cut a piece long enough to stretch across the forehead and about 2 cm (¾") wide. Cut it into a fringe and sew it across the forehead. Cut two more strips long enough to encircle the back of the head from cheek to cheek. Cut both lengths in a fringe and sew one piece across the back of the head just above ear level and the other piece on the top of the head almost folded together so that the join makes a parting and the fringed side covers the top of the lower fringed piece.

Kewpie doll

This larger-size, flat felt doll has a slightly different shape. The arms stand out to the side and the hands are shaped with a suggestion of a thumb, like a Kewpie doll.

You will need:

Felt; embroidery silks; wool or silk for hair; some kapok or other soft stuffing.

This one too can be sewn up either with stab stitch or oversewing. If stab-stitching it, then fold the felt in half and trace the template (Fig 8) once on to one half and tack the two pieces together round the outside of the shape. Do not cut off any of the surplus material until the sewing is completed.

Leave one side of the doll open for stuffing. Complete the stuffing and sewing up as for the other doll, remembering to keep it flat rather than round because it is in only two pieces.

Embroider features in coloured silks or wool, or cut shapes for eyes and mouth from felt, and sew on wool for hair.

Kewpie doll with head gusset

A doll with a rounder head can also be made from this same template out of pale flesh-coloured felt, by sewing in a gusset over the head from one side of the neck to the other.

Measure the distance and cut a strip of felt this length, about 2 cm (¾") wide in the middle and tapering to a point at each end.

Sew the gusset to both of the head pieces, taking care to match starting and finishing points exactly. Sew up the rest of the doll, leaving an opening. Finish the stuffing and sewing up as before.

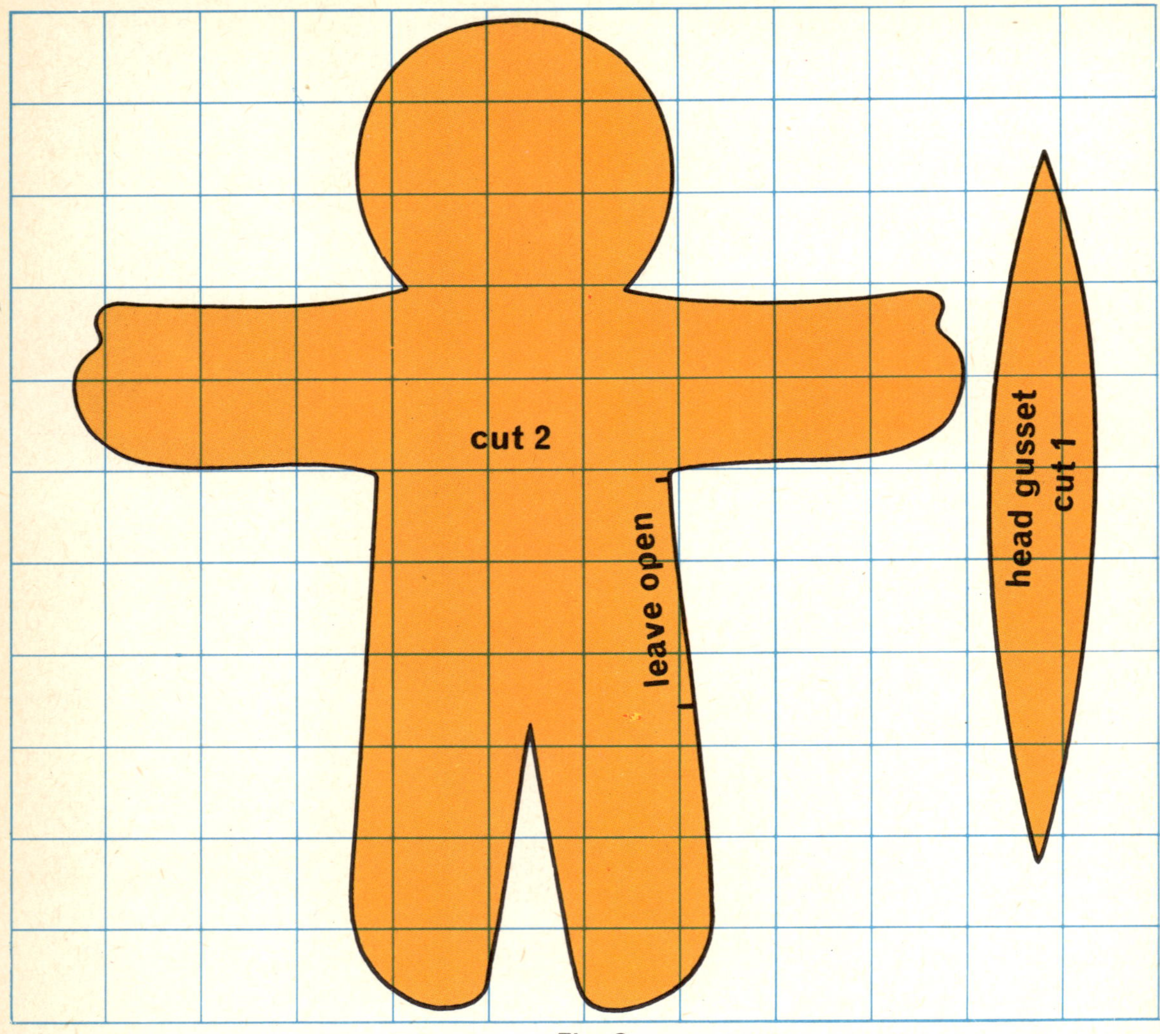

Fig 8

Mexican peon doll

in the picture is made up and finished off exactly like the other dolls.

For his clothes you will need:

Reddish-brown felt for the doll; white felt or other material for trousers; red felt for waistcoat; soft white nylon or cambric for blouse; tiny pearl buttons; lace; ribbon; silver ricrac braid; kapok; natural-coloured raffia; a medium crochet hook; black embroidery silk and cotton.

Cut this blouse with very full sleeves gathered into the wrists, with a frill of narrow lace and tiny pearl buttons down the front.

To cut it, measure from the tip of one hand to the other, and from the top of the shoulder to below the waist, and fold a piece of cambric to these measurements (Fig 9). Measure from side to side of the waist, allow an extra 2.5 cm (1'') for turnings and cut out the triangle from each lower corner (Fig 10), the fold of the material being at the top. Turn it inside out, sew the seams and gather up the wrists with a narrow turning. Cut down the front from neck to hem and sew lace and buttons down one side; make a turning at neck and hem.

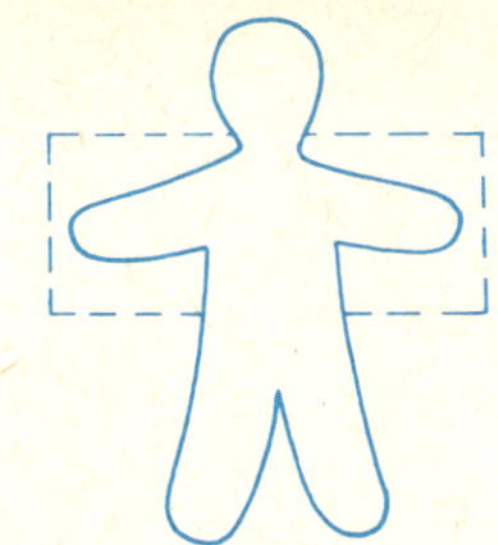

Fig 9

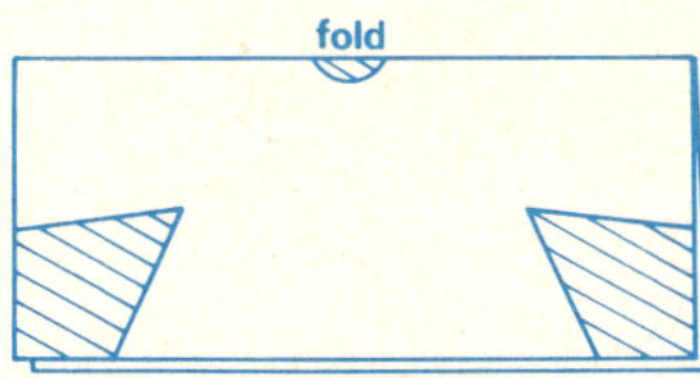

Fig 10

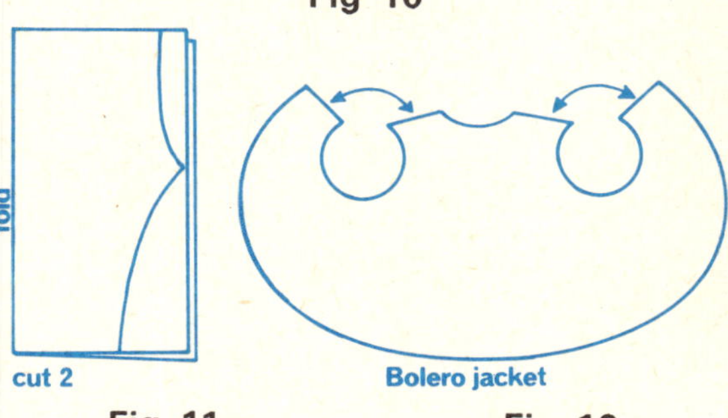

Fig 11

Fig 12

The trousers

Measure from waist to foot for length and all round the waist for width, allowing extra for turnings if not using felt. Cut two pieces (Fig 11). Sew the two leg seams, then sew the seam joining the two fronts and backs from the waist in front to the waist at the back. Make small turnings on the legs and waist. Finish off round the waist with a narrow fringed ribbon sash.

Waistcoat jacket

Make this in red felt with a curved front, buttonholed round the edges and with stripes of silver ricrac braid sewn across the fronts (Fig 12).

Features

His features are worked in black embroidery silk, eyes narrow and rather slit-like, and three or four strands to make a drooping, thin moustache. His hair is worked with thick black embroidery cotton in long and short straight stitches.

Hat

His pointed, wide-brimmed hat is crocheted from natural-coloured raffia, starting with the brim, making a big ring of chain, and working double crochet into every stitch without decreasing until about 2 cm (¾''), then decreasing until it fits his head. Decrease very gradually for the crown until very few stitches are left. Sew them all together.

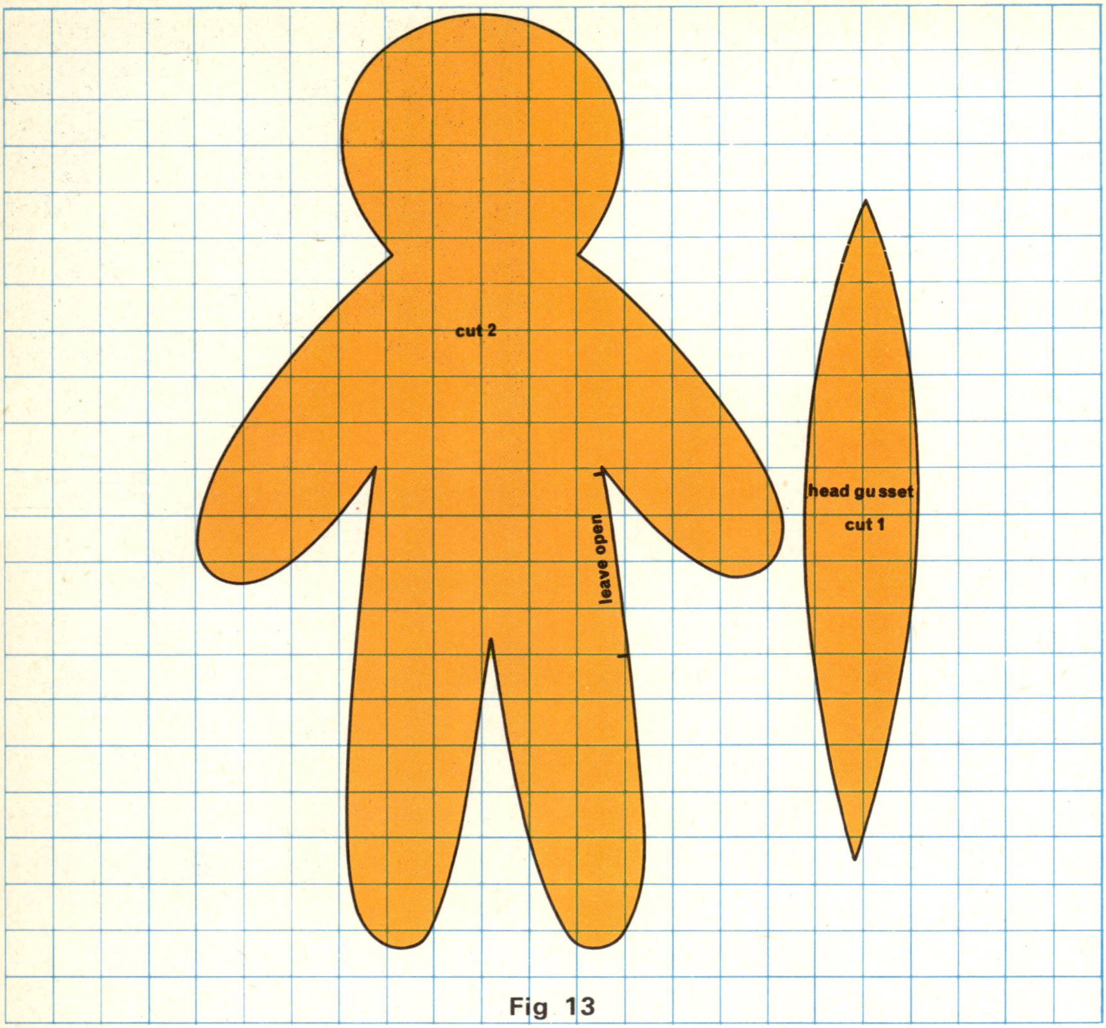
cut 2
leave open
head gusset
cut 1

Fig 13

61 cm (24'') square

Fig 14

fold
cut away shaded part

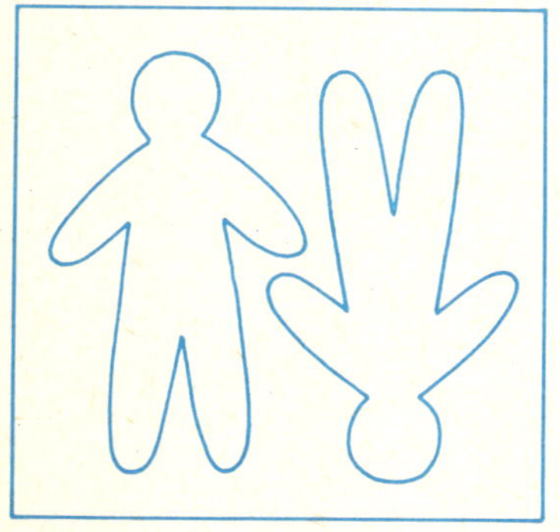

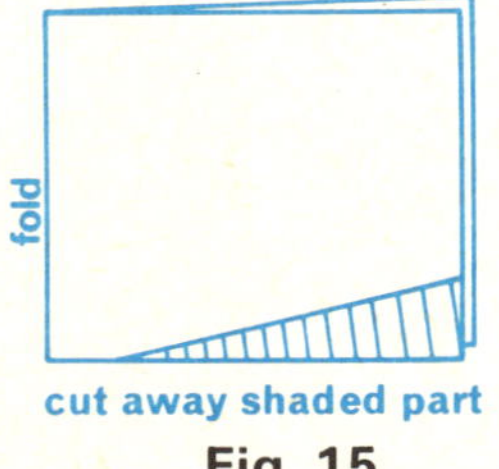

Fig 15

Two larger dolls

Here are two larger felt dolls. Both can be made in two pieces rather flat, or with their heads rounder and more plump by inserting a gusset from one side of the neck over the head to the other side.

Little girl doll

The first doll (Fig 13) is a more natural little girl shape with the arms pointing down to the sides. When finished she is about 50 cm (20'') high. Cut the head gusset as in the other dolls with head gussets, but make this one about 3.5 cm to 5 cm (1¾'' to 2'') wide in the middle. (Vary the width of the gusset according to the size of the doll).

Sew the doll in the same way as for the little ones, which were given in detail.

Be careful not to stuff the doll too hard if not inserting a gusset, or all the seams at the edges will pucker.

You will need:

A 61 cm (24'') square of felt in natural or flesh colour to cut the doll, fitting in the template by turning it upside down and reversing it for the second piece (Fig 14).

The gusset, if used, will fit in over the pieces if you place them near the edge of the felt.

As she is a bigger doll her clothes can be made to take off and on, so that she can have a change of wardrobe. You will find too that the first-size knitting patterns for baby clothes will fit her.

Doll's clothes

For panties you will need: a piece of cotton material 18 cm by 21 cm (7'' by 8½'').

Fold it in half lengthways and then in half across the width, so that the long fold is at the left side and the other fold in front of you (Fig 15). Cut off the corner as shown, open it out and seam the two sides. Make a half-inch hem at the top and insert elastic. Make narrow hems on the legs, and add a frill of lace or embroidery.

Another shape of knickers can be made by folding the material (Fig 16) and cutting up the long fold for 1.25 cm to 2 cm (½'' to ¾''). Then sew the side seams and the inner leg seams and finish off in the same way as for the panties.

The dress

A dress with a gathered skirt and a belt or sash round the waist can be made from any cotton, gingham or silk material. The bodice is cut from two pieces of material one 16 cm by 15 cm (6½'' by 6'') for the front, and 21 cm by 15 cm (8½'' by 6'') for the two backs.

Fold both pieces in half lengthways and cut out the neck and armholes (Fig 17). The wide neck line in the piece for the backs is to allow for turnings on the back opening. Cut down the fold in the back.

Sew the side and shoulder seams. Make a turning on the neck and bind it with bias binding. Turn in 2.5 cm (1'') on each back fastening. Make a small turning on the armholes and sew a frill of ribbon or lace round each one.

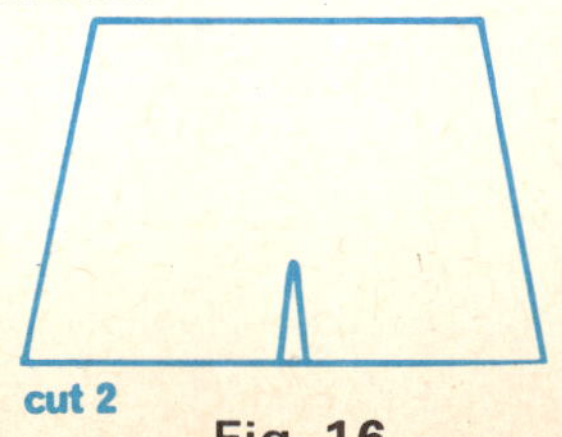

Fig 16

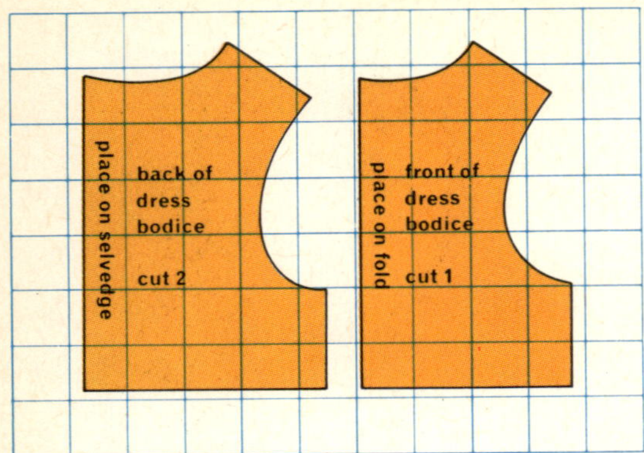

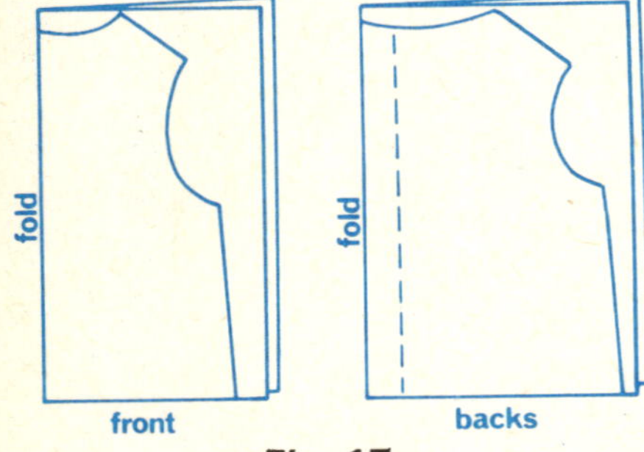

Fig 17

Skirt

The skirt is a straight strip of the same material cut to the length you wish (measuring from the waist and allowing extra for turnings) and about 61 cm to 76 cm (24″ to 30″) wide.

Join the seam (which will be at the back), leaving a quarter of it open. Make a hem along the bottom edge and embroider it with a decorative running stitch, or sew on braid or coloured tape.

Gather or pleat the other edge to fit the waist of the bodice and sew them together.

Sew press studs at neck, waist and the middle of the back opening.

Finish off the waist with a tie belt of the material, or coloured binding or ribbon.

Boots, mini dress and jumpsuit

Patterns for these are given in Fig 18.

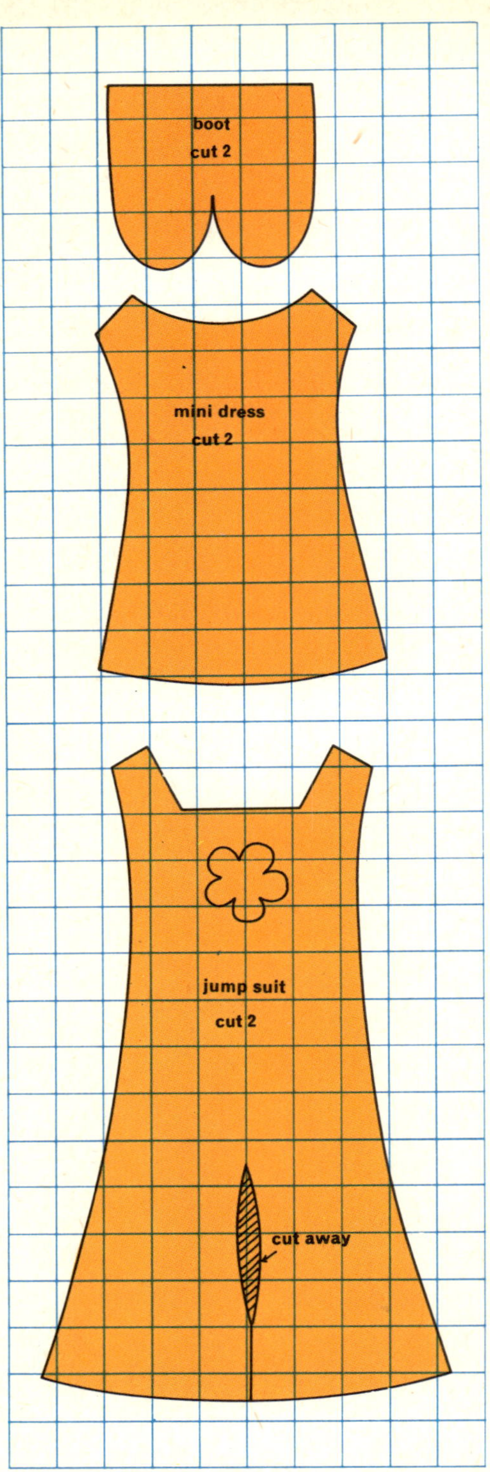

Fig 18

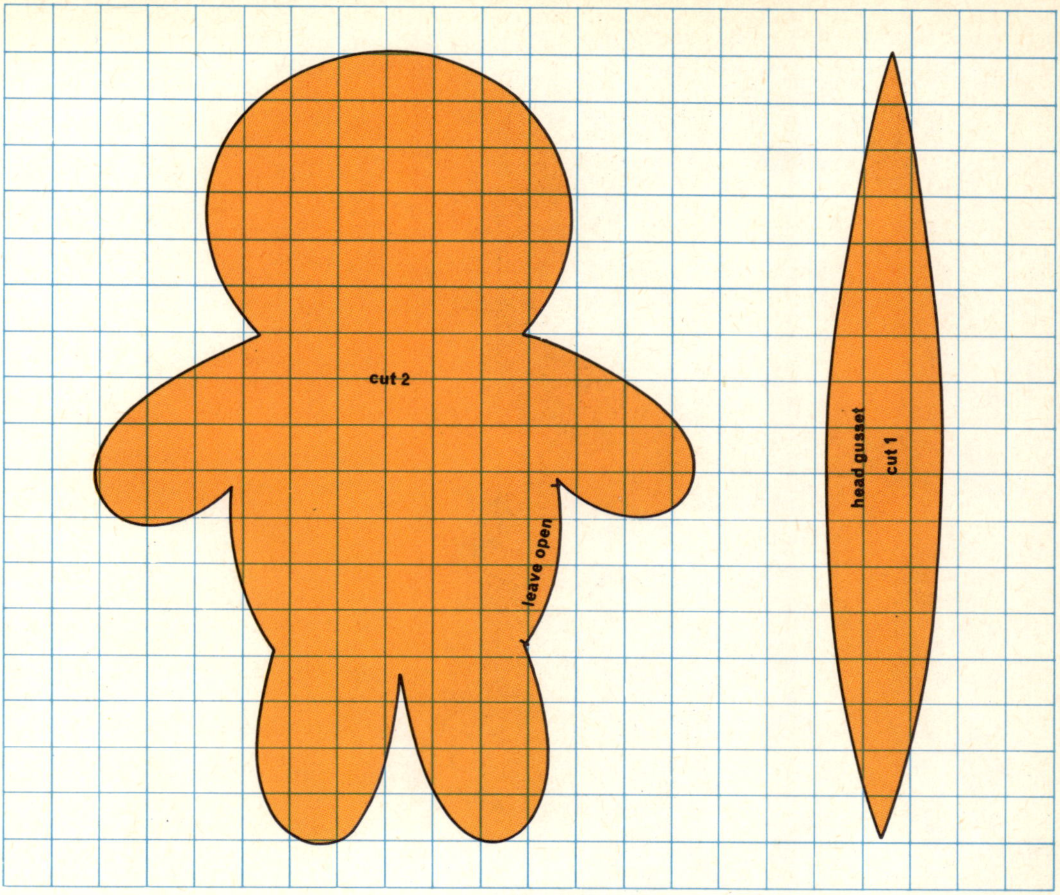

Fig 19

Baby doll

The second doll (Fig 19) with its short, fat little body and large head makes a very good baby doll. It, too, can be made in two pieces and flat, or have a gusset inserted in the head to make it rounder. It looks better with the gusset, but be careful not to make the gusset too wide in the middle because of the size of the head.

Features

When embroidering the features, set them in the lower half of the face to give it a real baby look. Make its hair in soft fair or brown curls (Fig 20). Thread a needle with the wool, take a stitch on the previously marked hair line along the forehead, place a finger close to it and wind the wool round it three or four times. Sew all the loops together to the

Fig 20

head, and continue making and sewing loops fairly close together all along the forehead and over the rest of the head.

Clothes

Little panties can be made from the previous doll's pattern and you can make an easy Spanish bib dress for her from a straight strip of material about 76 cm (30") wide, the length according to the measurement from neck to knee plus turnings (about 6 cm (2½") extra).

Spanish bib dress

(see p 57 for photograph)

Fold the material in four and make a crescent-shaped cut from the folded side, curving up to the neck. This will make little cap sleeves (Fig 21). Make an inch-wide hem along the top with a heading and thread a ribbon through it (Fig 21a). Make a similar hem on the bottom edge but without the heading, and embroider it or bind it with a contrasting colour of bias binding. Either sew blanket stitch embroidery round the armhole edges or bind them with similar bias binding.

The bib can be made into a dress by sewing up the back seam as far as the top hem, leaving that open.

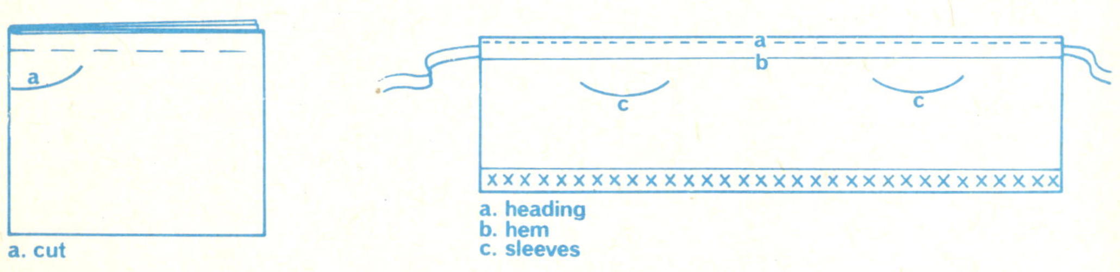

Fig 21

Fig 21a

Sock dolls

Jack and Jill

Jack and Jill here have been made from a very small pair of socks, the smallest size obtainable. You can make a sock doll from an old sock, which should be a white or pale-coloured one (it could be dyed pale pink) and it must not have any darns or holes in the back of the heel because this will be the doll's face.

You will need:

A sock; some kapok or other soft stuffing (old nylon stockings, cut up very fine); some wool to make the hair; embroidery silks; cotton for sewing; some pieces of felt or fabric and white lawn for clothes.

Cut off the toe of the sock across the instep (Fig 22) and fold the sock so that the back of the heel is on top and the cut instep at the back. See that it is folded evenly, and then cut up the middle of the ribbed welt to make legs (Fig 23). Turn it inside out and back-stitch round the legs (Fig 24). Turn it right side out.

Stuff the legs smoothly and back-stitch across the tops of the legs to give some movement and enable the doll to sit. Stuff the body and tie a thread around the neck. To make the neck and head firmer, fold a pipe cleaner in half, twist it a little and enclose it in a little stuffing in the neck so that half of it is in the body and half in the head (Fig 25). Be sure that it is entirely enclosed in stuffing. Stuff the head very

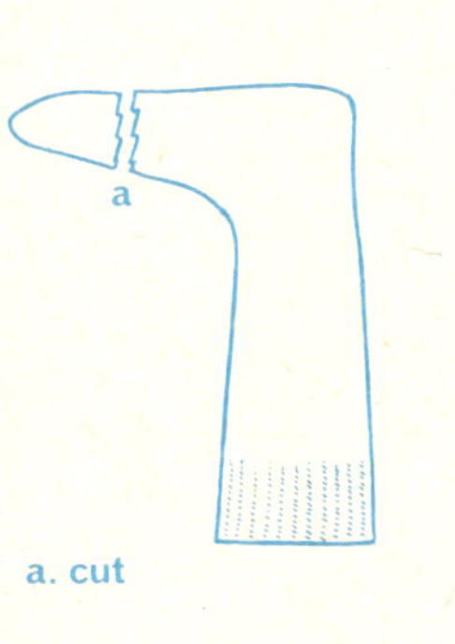

Fig 22

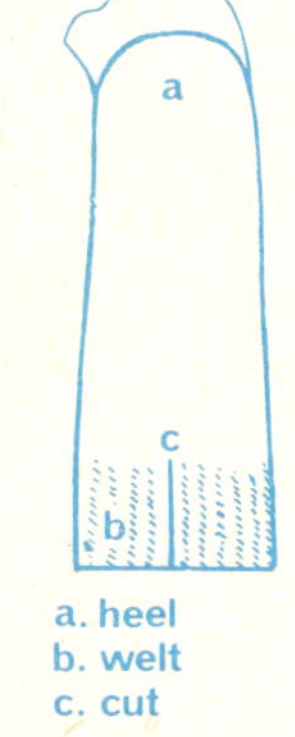

Fig 23

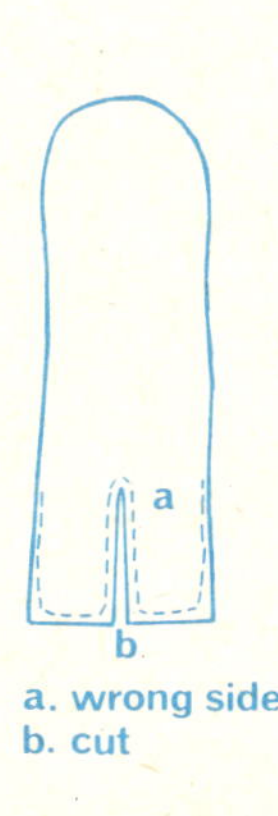

Fig 24

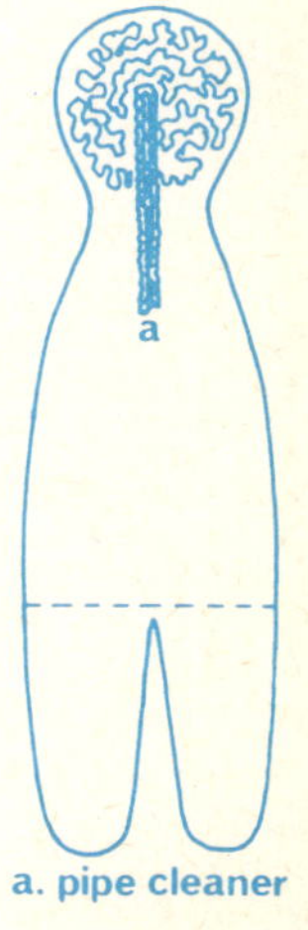

Fig 25

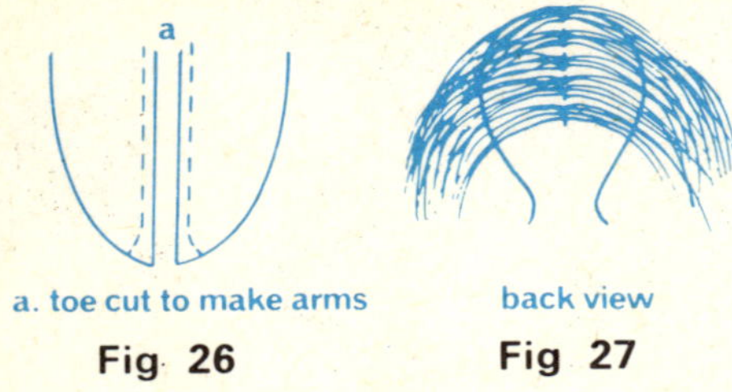

Fig 26 Fig 27

Fig 28 Fig 29

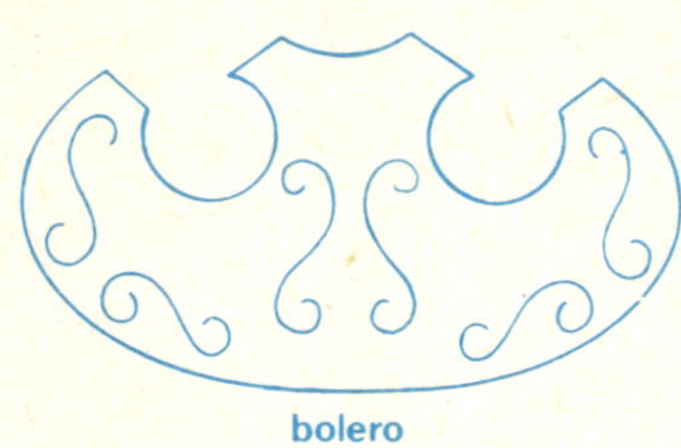

Fig 30

Fig 31

firmly, gather up the cut ends of the instep and sew them down at the back of head.

For arms, cut the toe pieces in half lengthways, turn them inside out and back-stitch (Fig 26). Turn right side out, stuff them, not too hard at the top, and sew them on across the shoulders.

Both boy and girl dolls are made in the same way.

Features

Embroider the features with embroidery silks or cotton. Drawing or painting them on the sock fabric is not very successful because the result is generally smudgy.

Jill

Hair

Jill's hair is yellow wool. A fringe of straight stitches is sewn on the forehead. For her plaits, cut ten or twelve strands of wool long enough to reach from her waist at one side, over the top of her head to her waist at the other side. Lay these across the head and sew down the middle parting with back-stitch (Fig 27). Plait them to fall each side of the face.

Dress

She is dressed in felt; her apron, embroidered jacket and cap giving her an Austrian or Swiss look.

The skirt is a straight piece of felt, embroidered at the hem and gathered round the waist (Fig 28).

A small rectangle of contrasting coloured felt makes the apron, embroidered at the bottom and sides and sewn over the skirt at the waist (Fig 29).

Little gathered white sleeves made from straight strips of white lawn are sewn on at the shoulders.

Jacket

The jacket or bolero is cut in one piece of black felt, embroidered in a scroll design on front and back and joined at the shoulders (Fig 30). The cap is an oblong of felt, folded in half to fit round the head, and the two sides oversewn (Fig 31). Sew it on the head round the edge with crossed oversewing in a contrasting silk.

Fig 32

Fig 33

Shoes

Her strap shoes are cut in two pieces, for back and front. Cut four pieces—draw a shape round the flattened foot—and cut out the centres of two of them (Fig 32). Sew the curved edges together, pull on over the foot and sew on round the top.

Jack

Hair

Jack's hair is embroidered in brown wool in long and short stitches each side of a parting (Fig 33). The second-row stitches are all the same length, joining with, and if necessary overlapping, the first row. Continue in this way until the head is covered.

Trousers

His trousers are cut in two pieces, the front with a bib (Fig 34) and the back to the waist (Fig 35). Sew a contrasting patch pocket to the front of each leg and embroider the bib in a simple design. Oversew the side seams and inside leg seams with contrasting silk and

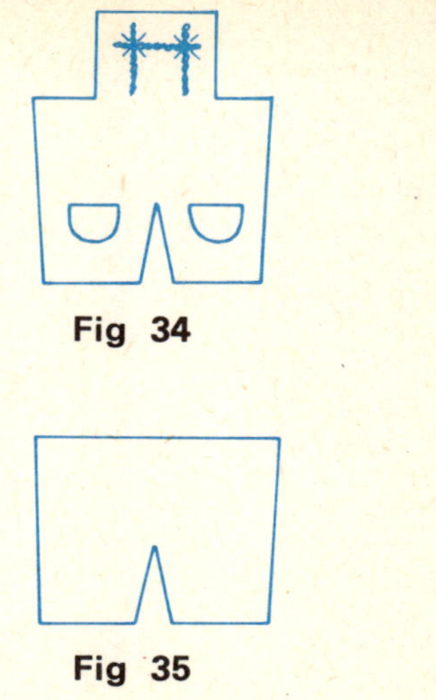

Fig 34

Fig 35

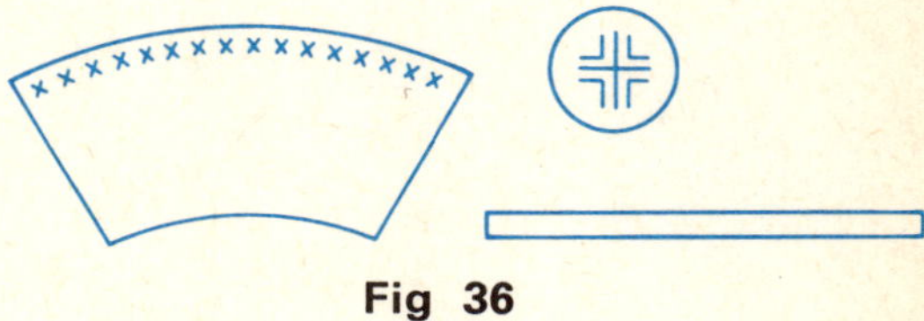

Fig 36

oversew the edges of the trouser legs. Sew them on to the doll round the waist. Cut two strips of felt matching the pockets, long enough to reach from the waist in front, over the shoulder and crossing the back to the trousers waist. Embroider the strips and sew them on.

Pail

The pail is made from a shaped piece of felt, embroidered along the top edge, and on the circle of felt for the bottom (Fig 36). Oversew the side seams, sew the circle to the base, and sew a strip at each side for a handle. Fasten it to the boy's hand with invisible stitches.

Fabric dolls

All of the patterns used for the felt dolls can be used for dolls made from fabrics such as calico, poplin, gingham or any other firmly woven material.

They can also be made from used material. Make quite sure that you use only the best and strongest parts, discarding anything which is thin or worn, or your finished doll will not last for very long, which would be a great pity after you had put so much work into it.

Trace round the templates on to the wrong side of the material, folded in half, and tack the shapes together outside the pencil edge.

Machine-stitch or back-stitch firmly all round the pencil line, leaving one side open for stuffing.

Trim off all surplus material, cut out small 'v's in all curved edges and snip into all corners, at neck, under arms and legs, as close as possible to the stitching, but without cutting it (Fig 37). If in doubt about the strength of the stitching at these points, do a second row touching the first or almost on top of it. Do not leave a space between the rows or the edge on the right side will be pulled too tight and will pucker. Turn the stitched and trimmed shape inside out, and press the edges flat.

Stuffing and make up is the same as for the felt dolls.

Arms and legs will move better if a row of back stitching is worked across the shoulders and the tops of the legs (Fig 38); these parts should be stuffed sparingly. A

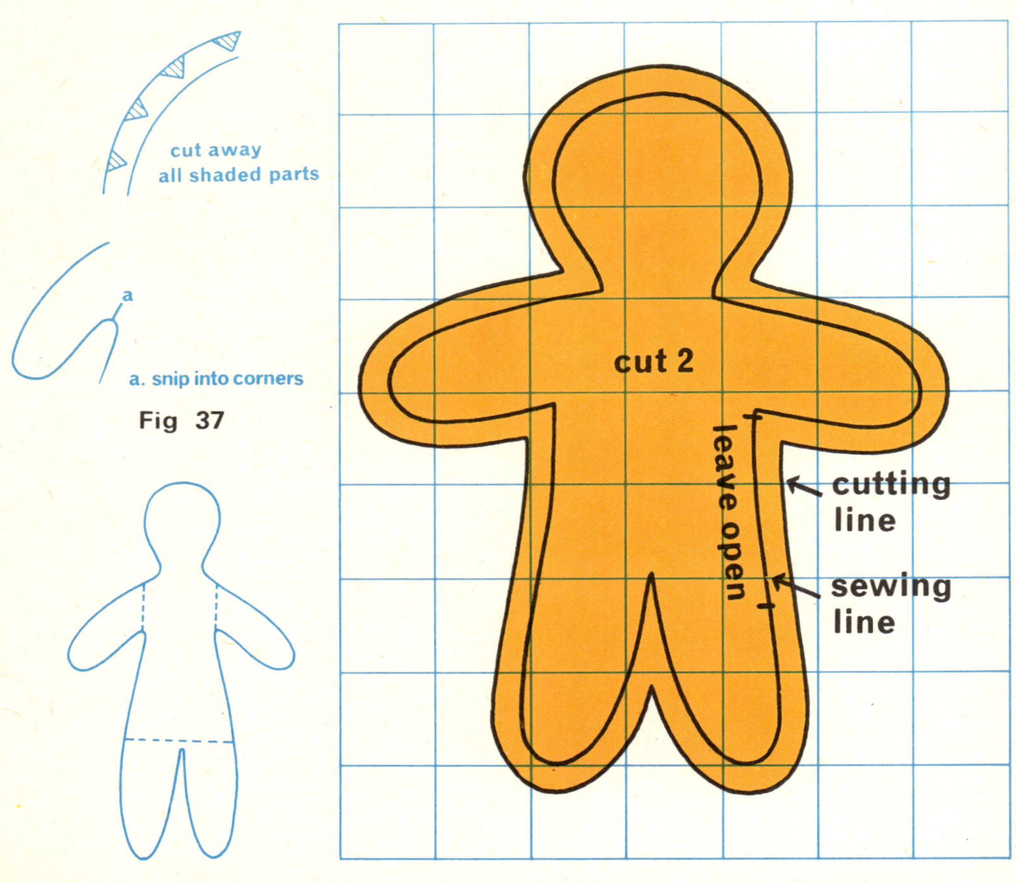

Fig 37

Fig 38

Fig 39

variation can also be made in the pattern to give a doll with more flexible arms, by cutting the arms separately, making them up, stuffing them—keeping stuffing thin at the open ends—and sewing them on across the shoulders so that they hang loosely at the side of the doll.

Small doll

This little one made in pale pink poplin can be made in just two pieces for a very easy and quickly made doll. Or she can have a head gusset just like the big dolls but, because of her size, the very small corners of the head gusset need careful manipulating. Because the doll is so small, too, it is easier to sew by hand than by machine. (Template Fig 39).

If you are machining, allow generous turnings and tack the pieces together very firmly outside the pencilled line. If sewing by hand, use a small back-stitch or double running stitch, which is done by doing a second row of running stitch over the first one, in the spaces.

Snip 'v's in all curves, and snip into the corners very carefully. Trim off all the surplus turnings before turning it inside out.

Use a little blunted skewer for pushing small pieces of stuffing into legs and arms and take care not to pull too hard on the seams.

Finish off the features and hair in a similar way to the felt dolls. Felt-tip pens can be used quite successfully on these smooth-faced dolls.

Little panties for her can be made from a rectangle wide enough to go round the waist plus allowance for turnings, and length from waist to thigh (Fig 40). Make a small hem on one long side and sew lace on the other side. Join the seam and insert elastic in the top hem. Join the middle of the two edges of the lacy side to make the two legs of the panties (Fig 41).

The Spanish bib (see earlier) made into a dress is simple to make for the small dolls.

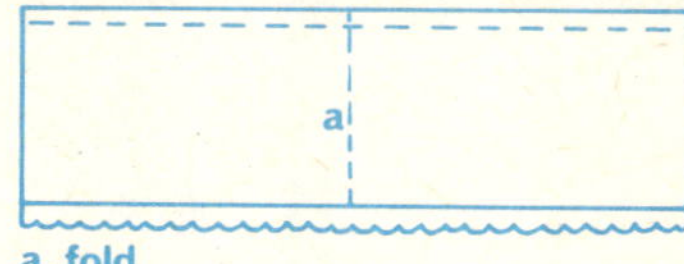

Fig 40

Fig 41

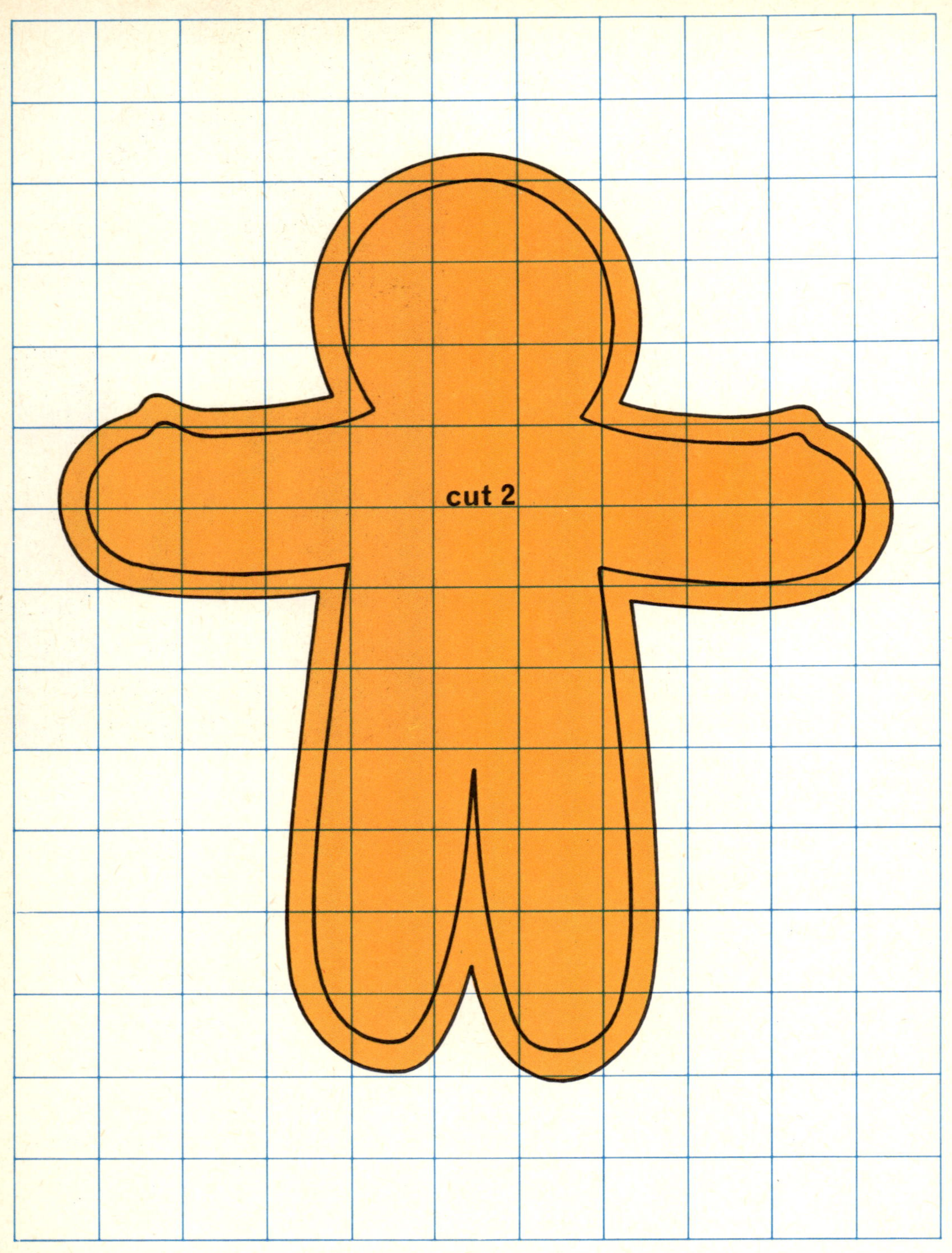

Fig 42

Medium-sized Bavarian doll

This is made from unbleached calico. The template (Fig 42) is traced on to the wrong side of the folded material, tacked together outside the pencil line and machined or back-stitched along the pencil line, leaving one side open for stuffing. It can have a rounder head by stitching in a gusset. Legs and arms can be jointed by stuffing thinly at shoulders and hips and either machining or back-stitching across the joints.

Clothes

The one in the picture is dressed in a type of Bavarian national costume. She is wearing thick, white, knitted, cotton stockings, which have been made from discarded cotton socks, and felt or bonded interlining shoes. Her black skirt is full and embroidered on the edge with braid. An embroidered white blouse with puff sleeves has over it a sleeveless bolero jacket, laced together with a coloured wool in the front. Her apron is patterned – it could be embroidered – and is lace-edged to match her head scarf, which is a triangle edged with lace to frame the face.

Features

Her features are drawn with felt-tip pens; the brows, lashes and mouth are done in embroidery silks. Her hair under the scarf is of strands of yellow wool sewn down with a centre parting and made into short plaits each side.

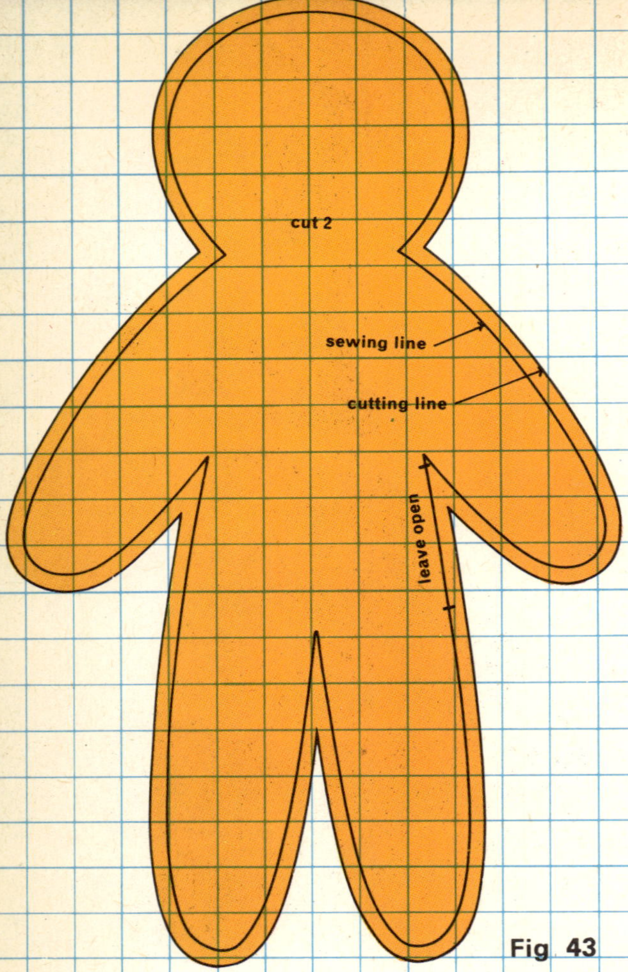

cut 2

sewing line

cutting line

leave open

Fig 43

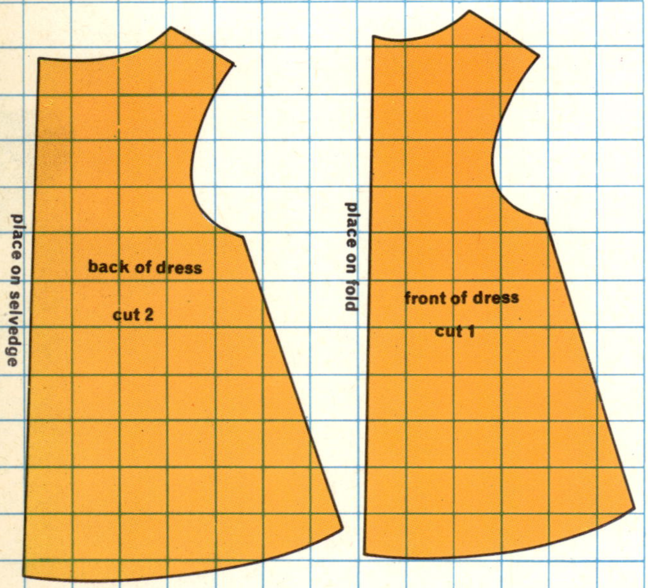

back of dress

cut 2

place on selvedge

front of dress

cut 1

place on fold

Fig 44

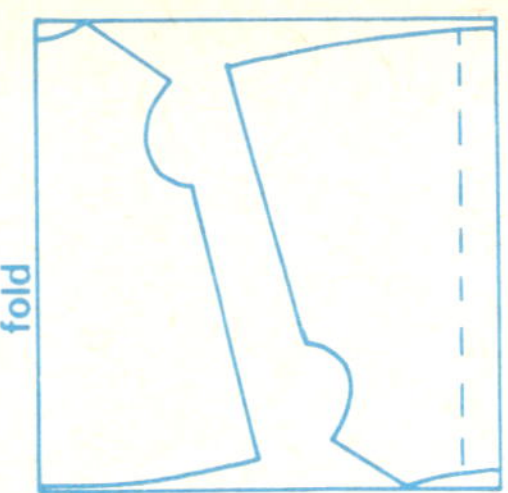

Fig 45

Larger dolls

These two bigger dolls can be made in pale pink poplin, with or without head gussets. One which measures 48 cm (19″) when finished (Fig 43) can be a little boy or girl doll. The other shorter one, 28 cm (15″) and more squat looking, with a big head, makes a very good baby doll (Fig 46).

A flared, skirted dress

A pretty, flared, skirted dress, fastened up the back with press studs, can be made from the given pattern.

To make it big enough for the 48 cm (19″) doll you must make your pattern four times bigger than Fig 44. The squares on this grid measure 6 mm (¼″), so make your grid of 2.5 cm (1″) squares. Mark dots on it where the lines of the pattern cross the grid lines and when the dots are joined up you will have the larger pattern.

Fold the pattern in half and cut it down the centre. Use one piece to cut the front of the dress, laying the straight edge of the pattern on the fold of the material, because the straight line will be the centre front of the dress. To cut the backs, place the straight edge of the pattern 2.5 cm (1″) in from the selvedges to allow a turning for fastening the

Fig 47

dress. If your material is plain, or with an all-over pattern which has no up and down to it, you can lay the patterns on the material as in Fig 45, which then takes less material – 23 cm (9″) of 91 cm (36″) width should do it easily.

Join the backs to the front at side and shoulder seams. Bind the neck, armholes and hem with bias binding and fasten the back with press studs. Sew a button on over each press stud.

The baby doll

Just a variation on the felt baby doll (Fig 46), but the features here can be drawn on the smooth surface with felt-tip pens. It is a good idea to practise drawing the features on a scrap of material – the same kind of material as for the doll and the same size as the doll's face – so that they can be placed in exactly the right position. Mistakes made with felt-tip pens will spoil the doll, so before painting or drawing the features make quite sure that you know what you are doing (Fig 47). Remember, also, to put baby features in the bottom half of the face.

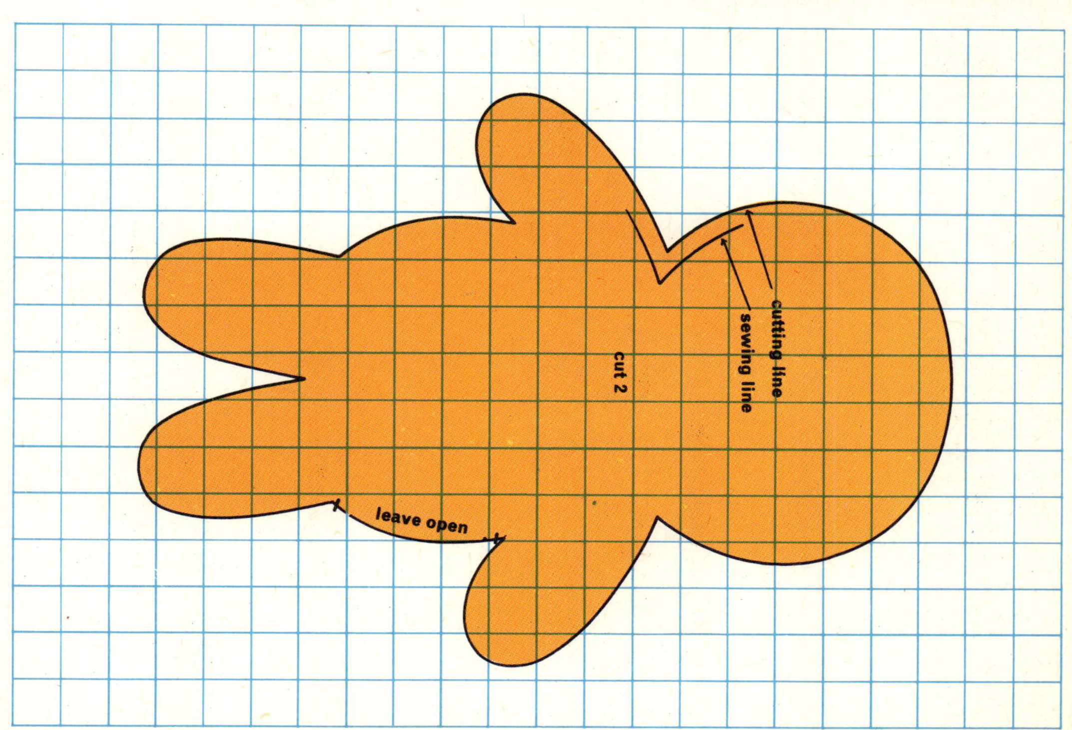

Fig 46

leg
cut 2
1.25 cm (½") turnings allowed
arm
cut 2
1.25 cm (½") turnings allowed
shoe
cut 4
body
cut 2
1.25 cm (½") turnings allowed
leave open
front of
bodice
place on fold
cut 1
back of
bodice
place on selvedge
cut 2
gather
sleeve
cut 2
gathered hem

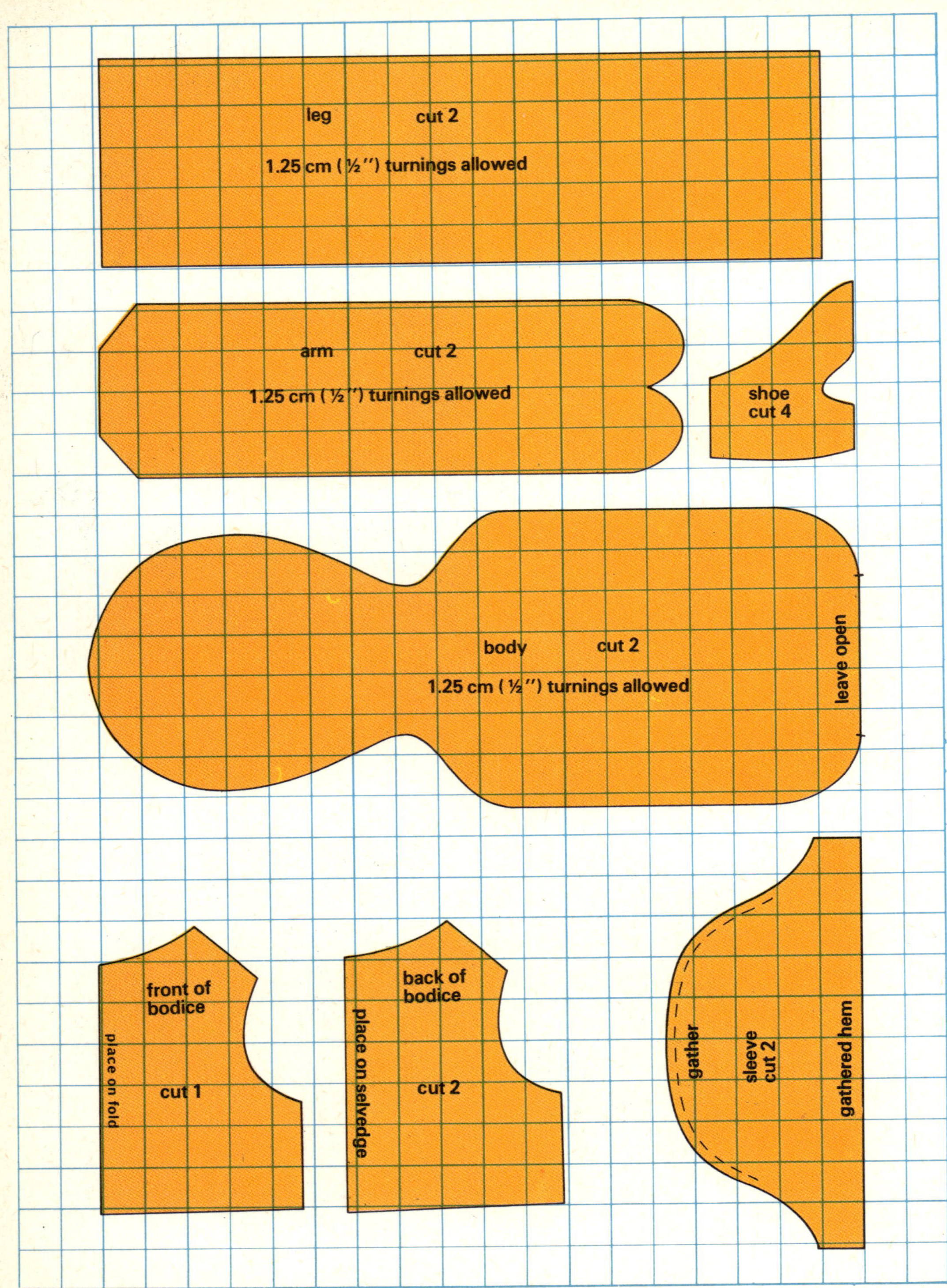

Fig 48

Jemima Jane *(Photograph on page 8)*

A Victorian miss with long legs and demure ringlets. She has on long lace-edged pantalettes, showing underneath her full-skirted, embroidered, check gingham dress, with short puffed sleeves and ribbon tie belt. She, too, is cut out of pale pink poplin (Fig 48). The pattern is in four pieces, body, arms, legs and shoes.

You will need:

Any smooth, closely woven material for the doll's body; 0.9 m (1 yd) of white cambric for pantalettes and waist slip;
2.7 m (3 yd) of narrow white lace;
1.4 m (1½ yd) of check gingham;
4 m (4½ yd) of medium width ricrac braid in white; 2.7 m (3 yd) of mauve seam binding (to match the dress, which is of mauve check gingham); some embroidery silks; kapok; blonde-yellow, thick, soft wool for hair; black felt or imitation leather for shoes.

Trace round the pattern templates on the wrong side of the material and cut out two body pieces, two arms, two legs, and four shoes from black felt or imitation leather. Allow turnings on the doll pieces when cutting them.

Machine or back-stitch on the pencil lines, leaving the bottom of the body open for stuffing, and the tops of the arms and legs.

Snip out 'v's in all the curved edges and snip once or twice into all corners (neck etc). Turn it inside out and press all the seams.

Turn right side out and fill with stuffing, not too hard, and sew up the openings. Sew the arms and legs in place. Sew two shoe pieces together for each shoe and sew them on to the legs round the ankle.

Pantalettes

Her pantalettes (Fig 49) are made from two rectangles of cambric 50 cm by 25 cm (20" by 10"). Fold them in half lengthways and stitch the side seams for 35.5 cm (14"). Pin the rest of the edges together from waist front to waist back for back and front seams. Make a small hem in the top and insert elastic. Make small turnings on the legs and sew on two rows of lace.

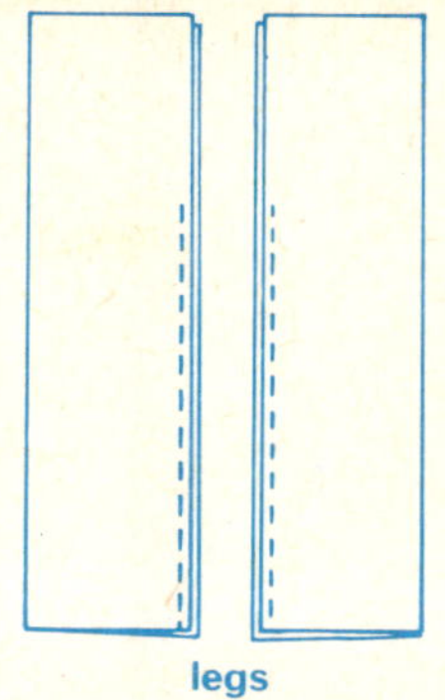

Fig 49

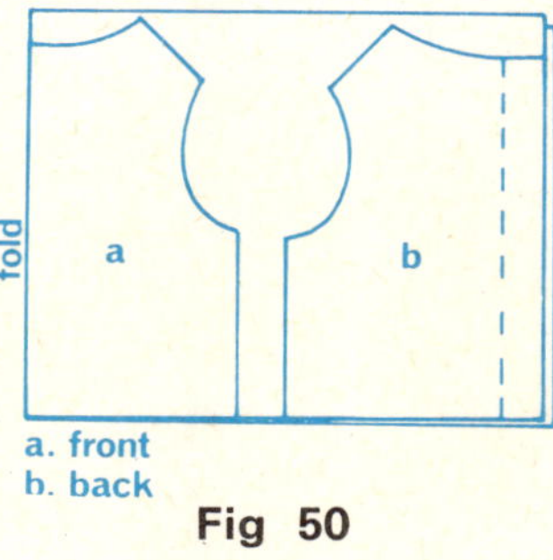

Fig 50

Slip

For the waist slip, cut a piece of cambric 40.5 cm by 68.5 cm (16" by 36"). Seam the two short edges. Make a small hem at the top for elastic, and sew a frill of lace all round the bottom edge.

Dress

The dress has a fitted bodice with a very full gathered skirt. Fold the bodice pattern in half and cut it down the middle. Place the piece for the front on folded material with the straight edge to the fold. Place the piece for the backs with the straight edge 2.5 cm (1") in from the selvedges (Fig 50). Seam the side and shoulder seams.

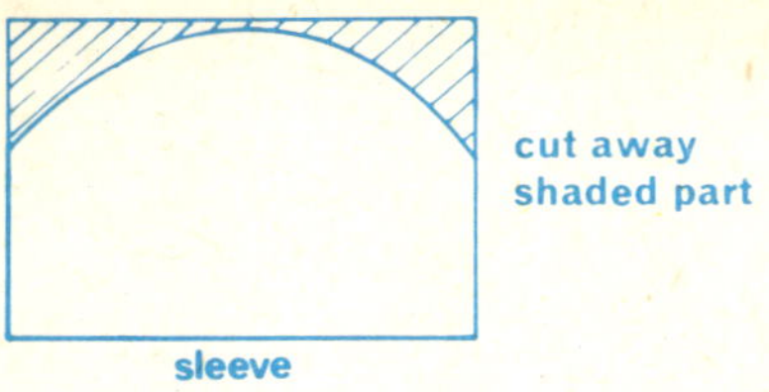

Fig 51

Fig 53

Sleeves

Cut two sleeves from folded material 16 cm by 46 cm (6½" by 18"). Curve the tops (Fig 51). Gather up the curved edge to fit the armhole and sew it in place. Make a turning on the bottom edge, gather it to fit the arm tightly and sew ricrac braid over the gathers.

Skirt

Cut two pieces of material for the skirt, each measuring 46 cm by 81 cm (18" by 36"). Join the selvedges together for front and back seam, leaving open 7.5 cm (3") at the top of the back seam. Gather the top edge and join on to the waist of the bodice (Fig 52). Make a hem on the bottom and sew a row of white ricrac over it on the right side. Sew a second row 6 cm (2½") above it and in between sew a strip of mauve seam binding with white ricrac on top of it.

Fig 52

Sew a 'v' of seam binding from each shoulder to the middle of the waist in front, with white ricrac on top of it (Fig 52). Bind the neck on the wrong side and sew ricrac round it on the stitching. Fasten the back with press studs, with pearl buttons sewn on top, and tie a strip of mauve seam binding round the waist with long ends in front.

Features

Embroider or draw features with felt-tip pens. Cut strands of silky wool long enough to reach from shoulder to shoulder over the head. Spread them over forehead and back of the head, sewing them down the centre parting with back stitch. Loop them over the forehead down the cheeks and tie in a bunch at each side of the face with mauve ribbons (Fig 53).

Stockinette dolls

Directions for making a doll from stockinette or vest material are given in Chapter Five. Different sizes of doll can be made in this material, just as in others, once you have the basic measurements. Dolls twice as big or half as big can be made by doubling or halving these measurements. Features on these dolls must be worked in embroidery silks or coloured cottons, not painted or drawn with felt-tip pens, because the material is not smooth enough and lines will be smudgy.

The little doll

Here in the knitted cap is a fun doll, both happy and sad at the same time, for one side of her head has a happy smiling face and the back (which is hidden by her hat) has a miserable, turned-down mouth and she looks ready to cry (Fig 54).

It is fun too to make an upside-down doll (Fig 55), particularly good in calico, by cutting out on double material two bodies joined at the waist, and four limbs. Dress both dolls in different characters as girl dolls, for instance, a schoolgirl at one end and a baby at the other. The dress of one doll will hide the other doll. So, you have two dolls in one and can have a quick change whenever you wish.

Fig 54

Fig 55

Dolls on wire frames

The little Indian prince riding on his elephant (in Chapter One) is made on a wire frame and the making is fully described there. He is small in size, and for larger dolls you must increase your length of wire, but the method of making them is the same. If you don't have a polystyrene ball to use for a head, then pad the loop of wire with wadding or screwed-up tissue paper, cover that with strips of soft material or bandage and finally with pale-coloured nylon stocking, which will stretch easily into shape. Pad the arms, legs and body with strips of material and finally with nylon stocking. Keep the loops in the wire for hands and feet.

The clown

Bobbing up and down on elastic, the clown has been made on one of these wire frames, but only his head needs to be padded because the rest of the frame is hidden by his baggy dress. Only his hands and feet are showing.

Fig 56

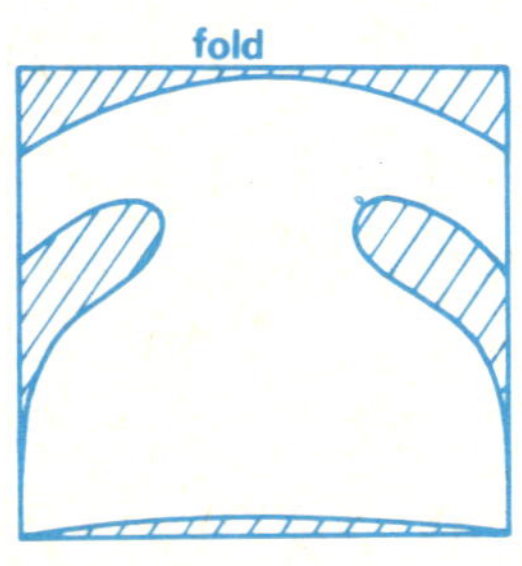

cut away all shaded parts

Fig 57

He can be made from pipe cleaners twisted together to make the required length, which is about 1.8 m (72''), but it is much easier to twist and form into shape if you have a continuous length of wire with no joins. The most comfortable kind of soft, flexible wire to use is pipe-cleaner chenille, which is like an extra soft and fluffy pipe cleaner.

The clown's feet and hands can be covered with old nylon stocking.

Features

His face has an oval, red felt mouth and a red felt nose cut as a circle. His eyes are embroidered black wool crosses and the eyebrows inverted 'v's of black felt or interlining (Fig 56). His pointed hat is cut from a segment of felt – about ¾ of a circle, the straight edges joined and the hat sewn on round the head.

Dress

His dress is cut in two pieces from two 20 cm (8'') squares, and cut as in Fig 57. Sew the side seams and shoulder seams, leaving a neck opening. Make a turning on the sleeves and gather them up. Make a small turning along the bottom.

Fit the dress on, sewing the neck closely to the wire and sew the front and back edges of the bottom together, sewing in the legs with it. Cut a strip of white Vilene, about 2.5 cm (1'') wide and 25 cm (10'') long. Draw blue and red stripes on each long edge with felt-tip pens, gather it up along the middle and sew on at the neck.

Hat

He could have wool bobbles (made like those for the pierrot in Chapter Three) for his hat, dress and shoes. Sew a piece of round elastic in his hat, with a loop to hold at the end, and he will bounce beautifully for you.

Two little dolls

Made from cut lengths of wire, so if you have some shorter pieces left over from making other things, you can use them up like this.

The first doll can be made from two pieces, a 50 cm (20'') piece for head, body and legs, and an 18 cm (7'') piece for the arms. Fold the long piece in half, make the head loop and twist the remaining wire together for the body, leaving the last 10 cm (4'') for the legs. Twist a small loop at each end for the feet. Twist the ends of the shorter piece of wire for hands, and thread it through the body twist, just below the head loop. Bend the right one to the left, and the left one to the right to lock them in place.

The second doll frame

Made from three short lengths, the head and body from a 38 cm (15'') length, legs from a 30 cm (12'') strip and the arms from a 23 cm (9'') one.

Make the head and body and leave about 4 cm (1½'') of the body wires untwisted. Make loops for the feet on the leg wire, mark the centre of it and twist the body wires round it, one on each side of the centre mark. Make the arms in a similar way to the first doll. Pad the head loops for a soft, padded head, or cut the wires, make a hole in a polystyrene ball and push in the wires.

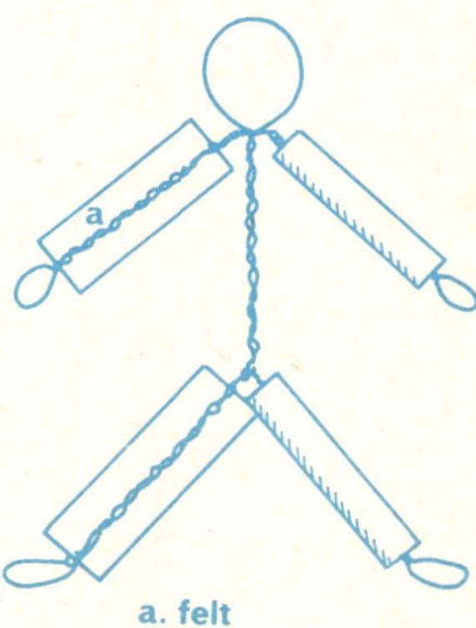

Fig 58

The small felt-covered doll

Made on the same type of frame, but legs, arms and body are covered with felt, which dresses him sufficiently, especially if a suitable colour of felt is chosen.

Cut two strips of felt 2.5 cm (1'') wide and long enough to reach from hip to ankle, and two similar strips for the arms from shoulder to wrist (Fig 58). Fold each piece round a wire limb and oversew the edges, turning the seams to the inside of legs and arms. Pad the body wire with strips of wadding or bandage. Cut two pieces of felt to reach

from shoulder to shoulder, covering the tops of the felt arms, and from shoulder to hips to cover the leg felts (Fig 59).

Sew the body inside these two pieces, oversewing the side seams and sewing in the arms and legs. Fold over the top corners on the shoulders and sew them down.

Pad the head and cover the whole with a piece of nylon stocking, tucking the ends down inside the neck edge of felt and sewing them in.

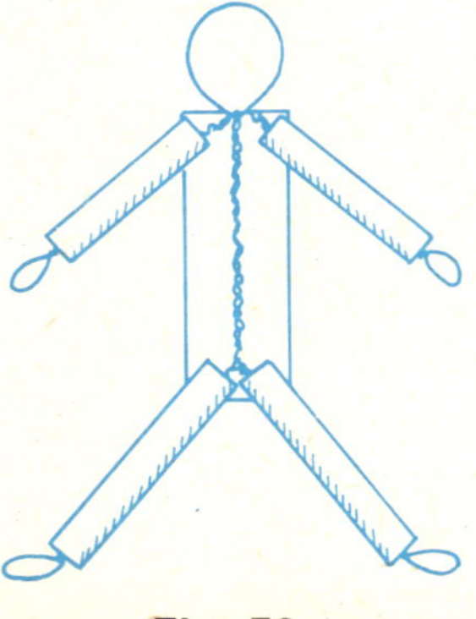

Fig 59

Fig 60

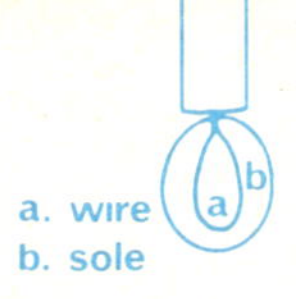

Fig 61

Cut four hand shapes in felt. Sew them together round the sides and fingers, slip them over the wire loops and sew round the wrist felt with thumbs pointing upwards (Fig 60).

Draw round the foot loop on a piece of felt and cut four ovals slightly bigger than the pencilled outline. Two pieces will be for the soles and two for the uppers. Make a small cut down the narrower end of the uppers and cut out a very small circle, only big enough to take the wire (Fig 61). Oversew the curved edges together, slide them over the slightly padded foot loops so that the cut-out circle fits over the wire. Sew up the back seam and sew the leg felt over the upper.

The four costume dolls

The Japanese lady, the Chinese coolie lad, the Pakistani lady and the Eskimo boy have all been made on wire frames.

Make your chosen dress by drawing the pattern shape you need round your finished doll frame, allowing good turnings.

Many books on national costume will give you ideas.

The Japanese lady

Her kimono, with its very wide sleeves, is in yellow thick silk, with a roll collar extending in a fold all down the front. Cuffs and lining of the wide sleeves are of grey and red striped silk and this also makes the obi—the wide sash bound round her waist in the traditional manner. Her inner sleeves and the neck band folded inside her kimono are of black and gold silk. Her feet have been padded and mounted on little leather soles, with thick black silk thongs to hold them on.

Hair

Hair has been stitched in long and short stitches in black wool with a big chignon of the black wool entwined with a black and gold band and a decorative pin thrust through.

The Pakistani lady

She has wide, swathed, green chiffon trousers, a blue close-fitting top and a long, filmy, green chiffon scarf across her shoulder.

Her hair is of long strands, to below the shoulder, of black embroidery silk, the face having been covered with a dark nylon stocking.

On her feet are little turned-up, pointed, Moorish-type blue felt slippers.

The Chinese coolie lad

He has long, black, heavy silk trousers and a kimono-type, hip-length jacket in blue, high at the neck and fastened with three red clips, with a rampant red dragon across the back.

His hair is sewn in long and short stitches in black sewing cotton, ending in a fine pigtail.

His hat is a shallow cone of yellow card, cut from a segment of a circle.

The Eskimo boy

He has had his wire frame well padded so that he appears to be warmly dressed. He has trousers and a longish coat with a hood in a furry white material banded on all edges and round the hood with a different kind of fur, and fur mitts on his hands.

His head has been covered with a brown nylon stocking and the straight fringe of hair showing under his hood has been worked in black wool. His moccasins are of thick grey felt.

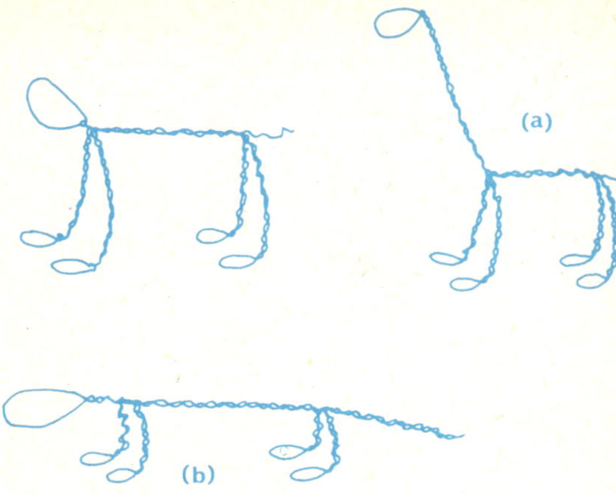

Fig 62

Animals

These wire frames, made in exactly the same way, can be used, with small adjustments, for many animals. These you might like to put with your dolls as pets. Or you can make a model or scene using several dolls and some background to illustrate it.

Dog

A dog can be made from the completed doll frame by bending the head up at right angles to the body (Fig 62), and the arms and legs down to make the animal's four legs.

Larger animals would need longer lengths of wire, just as the bigger dolls do.

Giraffe

A giraffe (Fig 62a) would need extra wire to twist into his long neck.

Crocodile

A crocodile (Fig 62b) needs extra wire in his long snout and body but less in his short, strong legs.

Dolls from old-fashioned dolly pegs (clothespins)

Whole families and sets of these little dolls can be made very quickly – in fact, as a wet holiday afternoon occupation it is a wonderful pastime.

You will need:

Old-fashioned pegs; some pipe cleaners to make arms; some scraps of material for dressing them; a little padding for the head; an old nylon stocking for covering the head padding and the arms; small piece of modelling clay to stand them on.

Cover the small knob with little pieces of wadding peeled in half to mould it better (Fig 63), or small pieces of kapok moulded round it, and cover it all with a piece of nylon stocking.

Wind a piece of wire round the neck, the ends forming the arms, with small loops turned over for hands.

Glue or sew on wool for hair, draw or embroider the features, and your doll is ready to be dressed.

In this little group of peg dolls are a ***little girl*** who is dressed ready for a party, in a very gay dress.

A cheeky-looking ***Irish leprechaun*** in long red trousers, bright green tail-coat and pointed fairy hat. His features have been

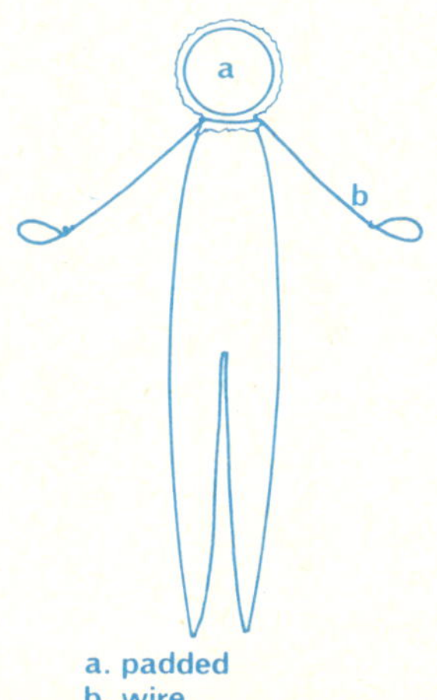

a. padded
b. wire

Fig 63

drawn with felt-tip pens and his beard of fine white cotton jersey stuck on. Little flesh-coloured felt hands have been sewn over the hand wires.

With him is a little lady from Russia.

The little ***Russian peasant doll*** has a very full-sleeved, gathered blouse and a full, gathered, green woollen skirt embroidered round the hem. Her apron is black and also embroidered. Over her yellow wool hair she wears a head scarf in green, embroidered to match the skirt.

Extremely dignified is the little ***Dutch lady doll*** who is really very grand in her best stiff black silk dress and apron. Her fichu and apron are of Dutch lace, as is her bonnet with its traditional ruched braid along the back. Under it you can see her yellow braided hair (of embroidery silk). In her hand she carries a jewelled net purse with a tiny silver Dutch coin. She is probably ready to go to church.

CHAPTER THREE

Knitted dolls

Points to remember

The basic plan for the knitted dolls in this chapter is a straight strip of garter-stitch knitting, the design so simple that small children can learn how to knit from it, the finished doll being much more fun to have than a knitted square for a pot holder or blanket or dish cloth.

The finished strip is folded over at the top of the head and joined up at each side. Knitting begins with the front half of the front legs, up the front of the body, the face and head, and then down the back of the body and the legs (Fig 1).

To make up the doll, fold the strip in half with the right side inside, and oversew the edges (Fig 2) back-stitching where the corners are to be rounded off for head and feet, and leaving an opening at one side for stuffing. Join the arm pieces in the same way, leaving the top open.

When changing colours in the knitted strip, be careful to make all joins of the new colours on the same side of the strip to give a right and wrong side (Fig 3), and in joining up be careful to match up the colours on each edge.

You can strengthen the neck of a knitted doll in the following way: fold a pipe cleaner in half, twist it, and insert it when stuffing the head so that half of it is in the head and half in the body. Keep it in the centre of the neck with stuffing all round it (Fig 4).

If a 'jointed' leg is required, then stuff the top of the leg thinly, back-stitch right across the top of the legs for a joint and the doll will be able to sit (Fig 5).

Other types of knitting stitch as well as garter stitch can be introduced, and the doll itself can be knitted in stocking stitch if wished.

Additions of clothes for dressing can vary in ply and make. In fact, this often adds interest to the finished doll.

In some cases three sizes of doll are given so that families of dolls can be knitted, and dressed. All sizes and directions for the medium and smallest ones are in the brackets. Small amounts of wool can be used for them, but the main body part should be made of the same ply and make of wool, otherwise the finished doll will be irregular and thinner in parts.

The basic measurements (Fig 6) for the whole strip for the dolls is as follows:

Front of legs: 11 (7.5; 6) cm.
Body: 35.5 (25.5; 18) cm, made up as follows:
body front: 11 (7.5; 6) cm;
face and head: 12.5 (10; 7.5) cm;
body back: 11 (7.5; 6) cm.
Backs of legs: 11 (7.5; 6) cm.

Abbreviations: k=knit; tog=together; st(s)=stitch(es).

Small children enjoy a change of colour and so a golliwog is quite a useful inducement for the beginner to keep on knitting.

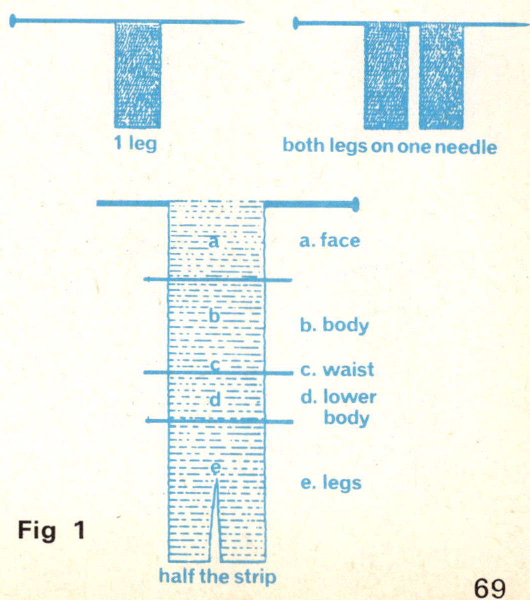

Fig 1

Golliwogs

You will need:

Approx ½ 50-gramme ball (1 oz) each of red, black, royal blue 4 ply or double knitting wool; three No 10 knitting pins; a pipe cleaner; scraps of black, red, white and yellow felt for trimming; kapok for stuffing.

NB. Colours must be joined on the same edge each time with the right side of the strip facing you. Directions are given for three sizes of golliwog but the amount of wool given here is for the largest-sized one only.

Legs

With black wool cast on 10 (8; 6) stitches.

Knit for 1.25 cm.

Change to blue wool.

Knit 10 (6.5; 4.5) cm.

Break off wool and leave sts on needle.

Knit a second leg to match and knit both sets of sts on to one needle giving 20 (16; 12) sts.

Body

Still with blue wool, knit 4 (2.5; 2) cm for rest of trousers.

Break off blue wool and join on red wool for jacket front.

Knit 7.5 (5; 4) cm and break off red wool.

Head

Join on black wool.

Knit 12.5 (10; 7.5) cm.

Break off black wool and join red wool.

Body

Knit 7.5 (5; 4) cm for back of jacket.

Change to blue wool.

Knit 4 (2.5; 2) cm for top of trousers.

Divide stitches.

Legs

On the first 10 sts knit in blue wool for 10 (6.5; 2) cm.

Change to black wool.

Knit 1.25 cm.

Cast off.

Rejoin wool to second 10 sts and finish second leg to match.

Arms

Cast on 16 (14; 12) sts.

Knit for 1.25 cm.

Change to red wool.

Knit 6.5 (5; 4) cm.

Cast off.

Knit a second arm to match.

Making up

Fold the strip in half with right side inside and take care to match the stripes of colour.

Oversew the head seams, back-stitching round the corners to round them off, and continue round the edges as in Fig 2, again rounding off the corners of the feet and leaving one side open for stuffing.

Turn inside out.

Head

Stuff the head very firmly, being careful not to stretch the knitting unduly, and insert a twisted pipe cleaner half in the head and half in the body, to keep the head and neck firm. Pad stuffing carefully round the pipe cleaner to keep it in the centre of the neck.

Tie a thread tightly round the neck.

Legs and body

Stuff the legs next, keeping stuffing thin at the top of the legs and back-stitching across the top of the legs to give them a 'joint'. Use a blunted pencil to push the stuffing into small openings like legs and arms. Stuff the body and sew up the opening.

Arms

Sew up the arms on the wrong side, rounding off the corners. Turn inside out and stuff firmly. Sew them on across the top of the shoulder.

Sew 1.25 cm loops of black wool all over the head, then cut the loops and trim the ends for a close mop (Fig 7).

Features

Cut two white felt circles for eyes and sew them on the face; cut a smiling crescent of red mouth and sew on invisibly.

Cut a belt and big buttons from black felt and sew in place.

Finish with a white felt collar and a big yellow bow.

The smaller golliwogs can have shorter trousers and striped jerseys for a change.

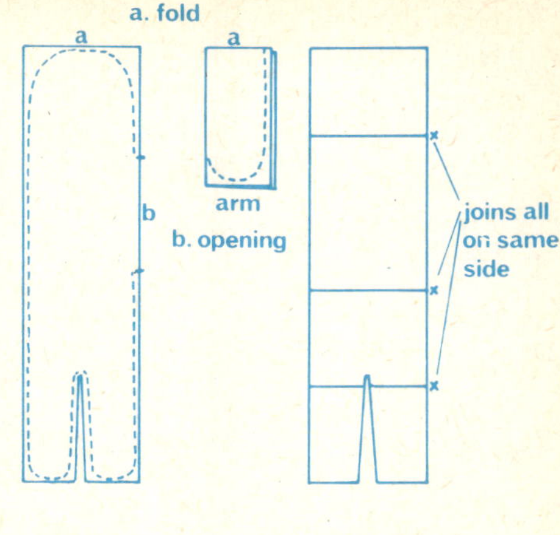

Fig 2 Fig 3

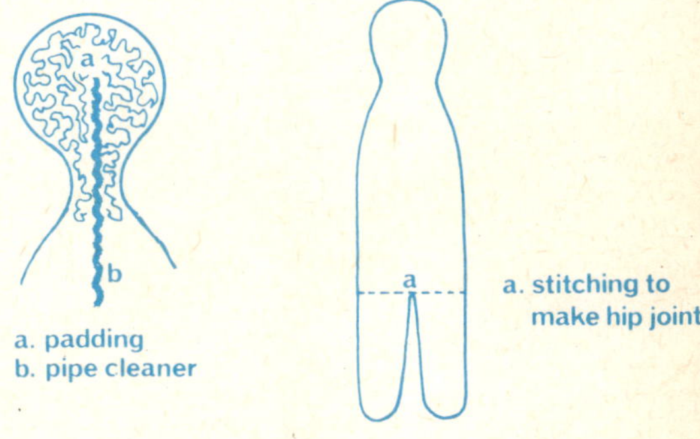

Fig 4 Fig 5

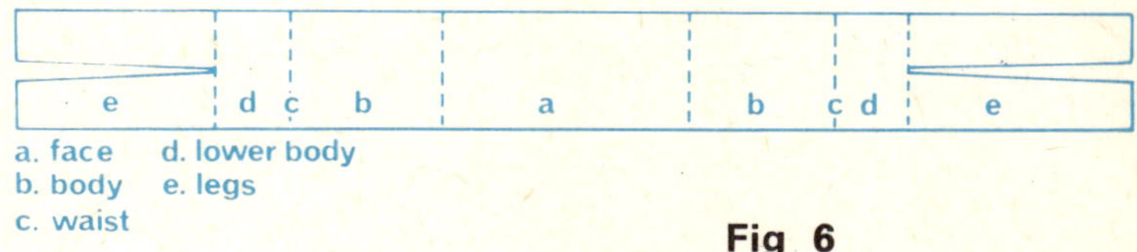

Fig 6

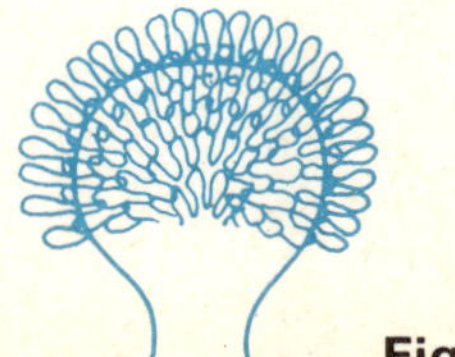

Fig 7

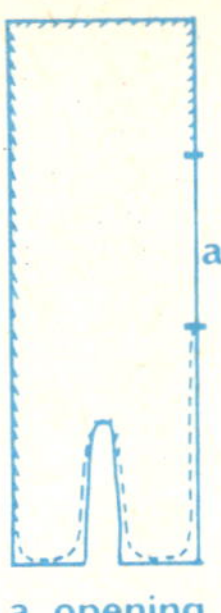

a. opening

Fig 8

a. corners gathered up for ears

Fig 9

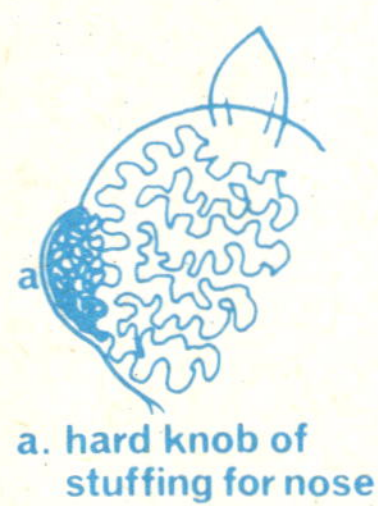

a. hard knob of stuffing for nose

Fig 10

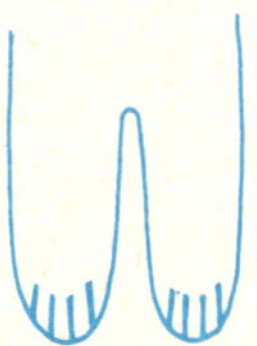

Fig 11

The Three Bears

You will need:

Approx 2 50-gramme balls (3 oz) of 4 ply or double knitting wool in a speckled golden yellow will make the set of three; three No 10 knitting pins; brown tapestry or embroidery wool; kapok for stuffing.

(Directions for Mother Bear and Baby Bear are given in the brackets).

Cast on 10 (8; 6) stitches.

Knit plain for 11 (7.5; 6) cm.

Break off wool and leave sts on needle.

Knit a second leg to match.

Knit both sets of sts on to one needle, 20 (16; 12) sts.

Knit plain on these sts for 35 (25; 19) cm.

Divide for the legs and on the first 10 (8; 6) sts knit 11 (7.5; 5) cm.

Cast off.

Rejoin wool to the remaining sts and complete to match the first leg.

Arms

Cast on 16 (14; 12) sts.

Knit plain for 7.5 (6.5; 5) cm.

Cast off.

Knit a second arm to match.

Making up

Fold the strip of knitting in half, right side inside.

For Father Bear put marker pins for the neck 6.5 cm from the fold.

(For Mother Bear mark 5 cm from the fold.)

(For Baby Bear 4 cm from fold.)

Oversew the head and leg seams and one side of the body, rounding off the leg corners for paws but not rounding off the head corners. Leave one side open for stuffing (Fig 8).

Turn it inside out.

Push the corners of the head well out and sew across the corners, gathering them slightly for ears (Fig 9).

Head

Stuff the head firmly to make a good shape, and then push a hard ball of stuffing into the front of the face to form a nose (Fig 10).

Finish the rest of the stuffing as for the golliwog.

Arms

Sew and stuff the arms. Do not stuff the arms too hard at the top and then they will hang at the sides instead of sticking out.

a. sequins

Fig 12

Fig 13

Features

Embroider a square block of straight stitches for the nose and mouth. Embroider the eyes, taking the wool from one to the other through the head and pulling slightly together to form features. Embroider lines in the ears to make them curl in, and straight lines for claws on each paw (Fig 11).

A pirate

You will need:

Approx ½ 50-gramme ball (1 oz) each of black, red, oyster wool in 4 ply or double knitting; a small quantity of white, green, yellow wool; a scrap of black felt for his eye patch and belt; fine silver metal-thread; three No 10 knitting pins; kapok for stuffing.

Cast on 10 stitches in black wool.

Knit 6.5 cm (2½″).

Change to red wool.

Knit 5 cm (2″)..

Break off wool and leave sts on needle.

Knit a second leg to match and put both on to one needle.

Knit 4 cm (1½″) in red wool.

Change to black and white wools.

Knit jersey for 7.5 cm (3″) in alternate stripes of black and white.

Change to oyster wool.

Knit 5 cm (2″) for his face.

Change to black wool.

Knit 7.5 cm (3″).

Knit the back of the striped jersey for 7.5 cm (3″), beginning with the same colour that ended at the neck of the jersey.

Change to red wool.

Knit 4 cm (1½″).

Divide for legs and complete them to match the front.

Arms

Knit 4 cm (1½″) in oyster wool and 4 cm (1½″) in black and white stripes to match the body of the jersey.

Head scarf

Cast on 2 sts in green.

Knit 4 rows.

Increase in the first stitch in the next and every 4th row till 20 sts are on the needle.

Knit 3 rows.

Knit together the first 2 sts in the next and every 4th row till 2 sts remain.

Cast off.

Neckerchief

Cast on 2 sts in yellow.

Knit 6 rows.

Increase at beginning of next and every 6th row till 12 sts.

Knit 5 rows then decrease at the beginning of the next and every 6th row till 2 sts remain.

Cast off.

Make up is the same as the golliwog; again, care should be taken to match the stripes.

Embroider the features with wool. Cut an oval patch in black felt and stitch in place for one eye. Cut a strip of black felt for a belt and sew on with a big buckle worked in fine silver metal-thread. Tie the neckerchief on with the two ends in the front. Tie the head scarf to one side with the ends over one ear and the point over the other. Sew a small ear ring on to one side of the head.

Puss-in-boots

You will need:

Approx ½ 50-gramme ball (1 oz) each of black, purple, yellow 4 ply or double knitting wool; approx ½ 50-gramme ball (1 oz) of lime colour in 3 ply wool, or in wool and fine metal-thread mixture; green, gold, silver metal-thread; strands of black wool; small feathers; sequins; two pipe cleaners; three No 10 knitting pins; kapok for stuffing; green and red felt.

Cast on 10 sts in purple wool.

Knit 5 cm (2'').

Change to black wool.

Knit 6.5 cm (2½'').

Break off wool and leave sts on needle.

Knit second leg to match and knit both sets of sts on to one needle.

Knit 35.5 cm (14'') in black, then divide sts and knit legs to match the front ones.

Cast on 16 sts in black wool for arms.

Knit 7.5 cm (3'').

Boot tops

With purple wool cast on 41 sts.

Knit 1.25 cm (½'').

Next row. K 2, k 2 tog, *k 4, k 2 tog.* Repeat from * to * to last stitch, k 1 (34 sts).

Knit for 1.25 cm (½'').

Next row. K 1, k 2 tog, *k 3, k 2 tog.* Repeat * to * to last st, k 1 (27 sts).

Knit 1.25 cm (½'').

Next row. K 1, k 2 tog *k 2, k 2 tog.* Repeat * to * to end (20 sts).

Knit 1.25 cm (½'').

Cast off.

Tail

Cast on 5 sts in black wool and knit 22.5 cm (9'').

Cast off.

Hat brim

With yellow wool cast on 80 sts.

Knit 3 rows.

Next row. *K 2, k 2 tog* all along the row (60 sts).

Knit 3 rows.

Next row.*K 1, k 2 tog* all along row (40 sts).

Knit 3 rows.

Next row. (**hat crown**). K 3, k 2 tog, *k 6, k 2 tog.* Repeat * to * to last 3 sts, k 3 (35 sts).

Knit 3 rows.

Next row. K 3, k 2 tog, *k 5, k 2 tog.* Repeat * to * to last 2 sts, k 2 (30 sts).

Knit 3 rows.

Next row. K 2, k 2 tog, *k 4, k 2 tog.* Repeat * to * to last 2 sts, k 2 (25 sts).

Knit 3 rows.

Next row. K 2, k 2 tog, *k 3, k 2 tog.* Repeat * to * to last stitch, k 1 (20 sts).

Knit 3 rows.

Next row. K 1, k 2 tog, *k 2, k 2 tog.* Repeat * to * to last stitch, k 1 (15 sts).

Knit 1 row.

Next row. *K 1, k 2 tog.* Repeat * to * to end of row (10 sts).

Knit 1 row.

Next row. K 2 tog all along the row (5 sts).

Run a thread through the 5 sts and fasten off.

Sew up the side seam.

Cloak

With lime wool and fine green metal-thread knitted together, cast on 60 sts.

Knit plain for 8 cm (3¼").

Next row. K 3 tog all along the row (20 sts).

Knit 5 rows.

Cast off.

Waist scarf

With lime wool and fine green metal-thread knitted together, cast on 4 sts and knit 22.5 cm (9").

Cast off.

Make a fringe on each end.

Make up the doll in the same way as the bear, sewing across the corners for ears and pushing a hard ball of stuffing in the front of the face for a nose.

Join the seams of the boot tops, and sew the narrow end on to the legs on the last row of purple knitting. Turn up the brim of the hat and sew a small bunch of curled feathers at one side.

Features

Cut two oval-shaped pieces of green felt and embroider all over with green metal-thread, or sew on green sequins (Fig 12), and sew to the face with a vertical bar of stitching in black wool.

Whiskers can be made from silver metal-thread. Thread this into a darning needle, insert the needle in the cheek and bring out at the nose, then take a back-stitch and bring the needle out on the other cheek. Repeat four or five times. Cut the loops of thread.

Embroider a few vertical stitches in black wool for a nose.

Cut a small crescent shape in red felt for a tongue and sew it on under the nose.

For the tail

Twist two pipe cleaners together to make a 24 cm (9½") length. Bend the ends back for 6 mm (¼"), and lay it on the strip of tail knitting. Oversew the seam, enclosing the pipe cleaner. Sew the tail on to the back so that it curls up the back and round to the front.

Tie the fringed scarf round his waist.

Decorate the boot tops with silver thread and sequins.

Embroider an order (Fig 13) on the left side of the chest with a sequin chain round the neck to simulate a decoration.

Sew on the hat with invisible stitches, giving it a sideways tilt, covering one ear so that the feathers droop over one shoulder.

Red Riding Hood

You will need:

Approx ½ 50-gramme ball (1 oz) each of red, pale pink, blue, white 4 ply or double knitting wool; a small quantity of black, brown, amber wool; four No 10 knitting pins; size 2.5 crochet hook; two pipe cleaners; kapok for stuffing; ribbon.

Cast on 8 stitches in black wool.

Knit 1.25 cm (½") for the front of the shoe.

Change to white wool.

Knit 2.5 cm (1") for the sock.

Change to pink wool.

Knit 7.5 cm (3") for leg.

Break off wool and leave sts on needle.

Knit a second leg to match and put both lots of stitches on to one needle (16 sts).

Leave them on the needle and knit the pantie frill.

Cast on 48 sts in white wool.

Knit 2 rows, knitting the first row into the front and not the backs of the sts to give a frilly edge.

Next row. K 3 tog all along the row (16 sts).

Knit the pantie frill on to the legs as follows:

Place the needle with the pantie frill on it in front of the one with the leg sts on it and knit together 1 stitch from each needle (16 sts).

Knit in white wool for 4 cm (1½").

Break off wool and leave.

Skirt

Cast on 40 sts in blue wool.

Knit for 5 cm (2").

Next row. K 2 tog all along the row (20 sts).

Next row. K 1, k 2 tog *k 3, k 2 tog.* Repeat * to * twice, k 2 (16 sts).

Knit the skirt on to the main doll in the same way as the legs were knitted on to the panties.

Knit in blue wool for 6.5 cm (2½").

Change to pink wool.

Knit 5 cm (2") for the face.

Cast off.

Repeat the above for the back of the body as far as the end of the blue wool for the body.

Join on the brown wool for hair.

Knit 5 cm (2"). Cast off.

Cloak

Cast on 60 sts in red wool.

Knit for 7-7.5 cm (2¾-3").

Next row. K 3, *k 2 tog, k 4.* Repeat * to * to last 3 sts, k 2 tog, k 1 (50 sts).

Knit 5 rows plain.

Next row. K 2, *k 2 tog, k 3.* Repeat * to * to last 3 sts, k 2 tog, k 1 (40 sts).

Knit 5 rows plain.

Next row. *K 2, k 2 tog.* Repeat * to * to end of row (30 sts).

Knit 5 rows plain.

Next row. *K 1, k 2 tog.* Repeat * to * to end of next row (20 sts).

Knit 5 rows plain.

Hood

Next row. *K 1, increase in next st.* Repeat * to * to last stitch, k 1 (30 sts).

K 7.5 cm (3") plain.

Cast off.

Arms

Cast on 14 sts in pink wool.

Knit 1.25 cm (½") for the hand.

Change to blue wool.

Knit 5 cm (2").

Cast off.

Knit a second arm to match.

Making up

Sew seams on the wrong side, leaving an opening for stuffing. Turn inside out. Sew up skirt side seams.

Stuff body and finish sewing up; stuff arms and sew on across the shoulder.

Embroider features, keeping them on lower half of face (Fig 14). Sew strands of brown wool across the top of the head, for hair, and finish in plaits at the sides of the face.

Seam the hood and tie the cloak round the neck with a ribbon.

Sew the hood to the head invisibly.

Fig 14

Fig 15

Fig 16

Basket

With amber wool and size 2.5 crochet hook make a ring of 4 chain and work into it 6 double crochet.

In the next two rounds work 2 double crochet into each stitch.

In next work 2 d c in alternate sts.

Continue working rounds with an occasional 2 d c into 1 stitch to keep the work flat, until it measures 6 cm (2¼") across.

Continue for five or six rounds without increasing, for the sides.

In the last round, work the stitches over a pipe cleaner to give a firm edge.

For a handle, insert the second pipe cleaner from side to side, bend up the ends and twist round. Bind wool all round it tightly to cover the cleaner. Attach it to the doll's arm with a few stitches.

Hawaiian girl

You will need:

Approx 2 50-gramme balls (3 oz) of light brown 4 ply or double knitting wool; black wool or silk for hair; three No 10 knitting pins; scraps of white and coloured felt; beads; raffia for skirt; kapok for stuffing.

For legs: cast on 10 stitches.

Knit 11 cm (4½").

Break off wool and leave sts on needle.

Knit a matching second leg, and put both sets of sts on one needle (20 sts).

Knit 35.5 cm (14") and then divide for legs, and knit them to match the front halves.

For arms knit 7.5 cm (3") on 16 sts.

Make up the doll as for the golliwog.

Skirt

Cut a length of wool about 40 cm (16") long. Cut the raffia into 25 cm (10") lengths (Fig 15), double each strand and knot it over the wool, pulling the two ends through the loop, and continue until it is sufficiently long to fit round the waist. Tie it tightly round the waist; secure in place with a few stitches.

Hair

Cut the wool or silk into 30 cm (12") lengths and lay it over the head from shoulder to shoulder. Spread it out over the back of the head and back-stitch it down the centre parting.

Cut simple flower shapes and leaves from felt (Fig 16) and sew in a garland round one side of the head and face.

Features

Cut two oval shapes in white felt for eyes and sew on with a flat blue bead in the centre.

Red felt or embroidery shapes the mouth.

Sew a small brass ring on the side of the head opposite the flowers.

Bead necklaces, anklets and bracelets can be made to match.

A guardsman

You will need:

Approx ½ 50-gramme ball (1 oz) each of black, red, royal blue, pink (pale) in 4 ply or double knitting wool; four No 10 knitting pins; strips of white felt; fine metal-thread; kapok for stuffing; 4 paper fasteners.

Colours must be joined on the same edge each time, with right side of work facing you.

Cast on 10 stitches.
Knit 2 cm (¾″) in black wool.
Knit 9.5 cm (3¾″) in blue wool.
Break off wool and leave sts on needle.
Knit a second leg and put all the stitches on one needle (20 sts).
Knit as follows on these 20 sts:
Blue 4 cm (1½″);
Red 7.5 cm (3″);
Pink 4 cm (1½″);
Black 18 cm (7″);
Red 7.5 cm (3″);
Blue 4 cm (1½″);
Here divide for legs and on the first 10 sts knit 9.5 cm (3¾″) in blue and 2 cm (¾″) in black.
Repeat for second leg.

Arms

Cast on 16 sts.
Knit 1.25 cm (½″) in pink wool and 6.5 cm (2½″) in red wool.
Cast off.
Knit a second arm to match.

Bottom of coat

Cast on 60 sts in red wool.
Knit 5 cm (2″).
Cast off.

Making up

Oversew all seams on the wrong side, leaving a side opening. Turn inside out and stuff. (Ease stuffing into arms and legs with a blunted pencil.) Finish sewing up. Stuff the arms and sew on across the shoulder.

Insert four paper fasteners down the front of the jacket for buttons.

Sew the bottom of the coat on at the waist, slightly overlapping the fronts. Cover the join with a strip of white felt for a belt.

Embroider a buckle with gold thread, and a red line down the outside of each leg in stem or back-stitch. Embroider features and moustache.

Cut a narrow strip of red felt to fit round the neck, embroider a motif each end and fasten it to the neck with invisible stitches, so that the two ends meet and the collar stands upright.

A sailor

You will need:

Approx 1½ 50-gramme balls (2 oz) of navy blue, approx ½ 50-gramme ball (1oz) each of black and pink, and a small quantity of white, all either 4 ply or double knitting wool; about 15 cm (6″) of narrow black ribbon; a black felt strip for a headband; silver metal-thread; four No 10 knitting pins; kapok for stuffing.

Legs

With black wool cast on 10 stitches.
Knit 7.5 cm (3″).
Break off wool and leave.

Bell bottom (See Fig 17)

With navy blue wool cast on 25 sts.
Knit 1.25 cm (½″).
Next row. K 2, k 2 tog, *k 8, k 2 tog.* Repeat * to * once, k 1 (22 sts).
Knit 1.25 cm (½″) without decreasing.
Next row. K 1, k 2 tog, *k 7, k 2 tog.* Repeat * to * once, k 1 (19 sts).
Knit 1.25 cm (½″).
Next row. K 2, k 2 tog, *k 5, k 2 tog.* Repeat * to * once, k 1 (16 sts).
Knit 1.25 cm (½″).
Next row. K 1, k 2 tog, *k 4, k 2 tog.* Repeat * to * once, k 1 (13 sts).
Knit 1.25 cm (½″).
Next row. * K 2, k 2 tog.* Repeat * to * twice, k 1 (10 sts).

To knit the bell bottom on to the leg, place the needle with the bell bottom in front of the needle with the leg stitches and knit together one stitch from each needle (10 sts).

Knit for 4 cm (1½″).
Break off wool, and leave sts on needle.
Knit a second leg to match, and put both sets of stitches on one needle (20 sts).
Knit 11 cm (4½″) for body, then 5 cm (2″) in pink wool and 1.25 cm (½″) in brown wool.
Cast off.
Repeat all the above for the second half to the end of the blue knitting.
Change to brown wool and knit 6.5 cm (2½″) for the back of the head.
Cast off.

Arms

Cast on 16 sts in pink wool.
Knit 1.25 cm (½″).
Change to navy blue wool.
Knit 6.5 cm (2½″).
Cast off.
Knit a second arm to match.

Collar (See Fig 18)

Cast on 16 sts in navy blue wool.
Knit 5 cm (2″).
Next row. K 5 sts, cast off the next 6 sts, and on the last 5 sts knit as follows:

Knit 3 rows.
On next row k 2 tog at the neck edge.
Knit 6.5 cm (2½") on these 4 sts.
Cast off.
Rejoin wool to the **neck** edge of the remaining 5 sts and knit 2 rows.
Next row. K 2 tog at the neck edge and knit 6.5 cm (2½") on remaining 4 sts.
Cast off.

Bib (See Fig 19)

Cast on 12 sts in white wool.
Knit 3 rows.
*Next row. K 2 tog at beginning and end of row.
Knit 3 rows.*
Repeat * to * till 2 sts remain.
Cast off.

Hat top

Cast on 8 sts in white wool.
Knit into the front and back of the first stitch in every row until 24 sts are on the needle.
Knit 8 rows without increasing.
Knit 2 tog at the beginning of each row until 8 sts remain.
Cast off.
Knit a second piece to match.

Making up

Sew all seams on the wrong side, leaving an opening at one side for stuffing and rounding off the corners for head and feet. Turn inside out and stuff. Finish sewing up.
Embroider features and a lock of brown wool over the forehead.
Sew and stuff arms and sew on to shoulders. Sew the bib to the chest under the chin.
Couch a line of white wool just inside the edge of the collar and sew it on to cover the edge of the bib.
Sew an end of the narrow ribbon each side under the collar and knot it in front.
Join the hat tops with the lines of knitting crossing each other and oversew the edges.
Cut a narrow strip of felt to fit the head.
Embroider the name in silver, join it into a ring and sew on the underside of the hat top. Fasten it to the head with small stitches.
Sew the side seams of the bell bottoms.

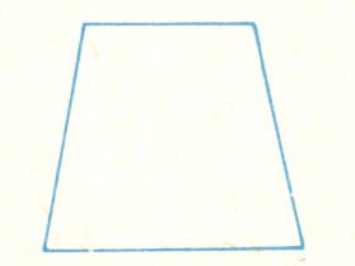
shape of bell bottom
Fig 17

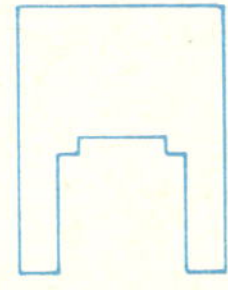
collar
Fig 18

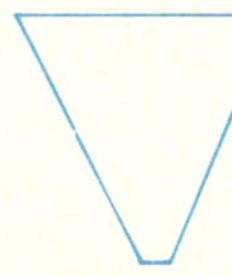
bib front
Fig 19

Father Christmas

You will need:

Approx 1½ 50-gramme balls (2 oz) of dark red wool; approx ½ 50-gramme ball (1 oz) each of white, black, pink, oatmeal-colour wool in 4 ply or double knitting; three No 10 knitting needles; a strip of black felt; kapok for stuffing.

Legs

Cast on 10 stitches in black wool.
Knit 6.5 cm (2½").
Change to red wool.
Knit 5 cm (2").
Break off wool and leave sts on needle.
Knit a second leg to match and put both sets of sts on to one needle (20 sts).
Knit in red wool for 11 cm (4½").

Join pink wool and knit 12.5 cm (5").
Knit 11 cm (4½") in red wool.
Divide for legs and knit them to match the front halves.

Arms

Cast on 16 sts in red wool.
Knit 7.5 cm (3").
Cast off.

Coat bottom

Cast on 54 sts in red wool.
Knit 7.5 cm (3").
Cast off.

Hood

Cast on 30 sts in red wool.
Knit 9.5 cm (3¾").
Cast off.

Sack

Cast on 8 sts in oatmeal-coloured wool.
Knit 1 row.
Next row. Knit into the front and back of each stitch (16 sts).
Knit 15 cm (6").
Next row. K 2 tog all along the row (8 sts).
Knit 1 row.
Cast off.
Make a cord or chain in the oatmeal-coloured wool to thread through the top of the sack.

Making up

Sew up all seams on the wrong side, leaving an opening for stuffing and rounding off the corners of head and feet. Turn inside out and stuff.

Sew and stuff arms and sew on at shoulders. Use a blunt pencil to ease the stuffing into the arms and legs.

Embroider thick white eyebrows and a bushy white moustache. Eyes are straight stitches in black wool.

Sew the coat bottom on to the waist, overlapping slightly in front. Cover the join with the strip of black felt for a belt.

Seam the hood along the top and attach at the neck.

Surround the face with two or three rows of 2 cm (¾") loops in white wool. Cut the loops and trim. Attach the hood to the face and head behind the white fringe.

Join the side seams of the sack, thread the cord through the top and hang it over one shoulder.

A Dutch boy

(see p 74)

His body is knitted in two parts—a front and a back.

You will need:

Approx ½ 50-gramme ball (1 oz) each of black, blue, red and flesh pink in 4 ply or double knitting wool; a small quantity of brown wool for hair; three No 10 knitting pins; kapok for stuffing.

Cast on 10 stitches in black wool.
Knit 1.25 cm (½").
Change to blue.
Next row. Increase in every stitch (20 sts).
Knit 12.5 cm (5").
Break wool and leave sts on needle.
Knit a second leg to match and put all sts on to one needle (40 sts).
Knit one row.
Next row. K 2 tog all along the row (20 sts).
Knit till work measures 16.5 cm (6½").
Change to red wool.
Knit 7.5 cm (3").
Knit 5 cm (2") in pink wool.
Knit 1.25 cm (½") in brown wool.
Cast off.
Knit a second piece to match, finishing at the end of the red knitting.
Join on brown wool and knit 6.5 cm (2½").
Cast off.

Arms

Cast on 16 sts in pink wool.
Knit 1.25 cm (½").
Change to red wool.
Knit 6 cm (2½").
Cast off.

Hat

Cast on 20 sts in black wool.
Knit 12.5 cm (5").
Cast off.

Scarf

Cast on 5 sts in black wool.
Knit 30 cm (12").
Cast off.
Make a small tassel and sew on to each end of it.

Making up

Oversew all seams on the wrong side,

leaving an opening in one side for stuffing, and rounding off corners for the head. Turn inside out. Stuff the body and sew up the opening. Sew and stuff the arms and sew them at shoulders.

Fold the piece for the hat in half, join the seams and sew it on to the head slightly at a tilted angle. Tie the scarf round the neck.

Embroider the features.

Ballerina or Christmas fairy

You will need:

Approx ½ 50-gramme ball (1 oz) each
of white and flesh pink 4 ply wool;
a small quantity of yellow or brown
wool for hair; three No 10 knitting pins;
some white tarlatan, net or tulle;
some silver cord; kapok for stuffing;
embroidery silk.

Cast on 10 stitches in white wool.
Knit 2.5 cm (1″).
Change to pink wool.
Knit 9 cm (3½″).
Break off wool and leave sts on needle.
Knit a second leg.
Put both sets on to one needle (20 sts) and knit 4 cm (1½″).
Change to white wool.
Knit 5 cm (2″) for the bodice.
Change to pink wool.
Knit 17.5 cm (7″).
Knit 5 cm (2″) in white wool.
Knit 4 cm (1½″) in pink wool.
Divide for legs and knit to match the front halves.

Arms

Cast on 14 sts.
Knit 7.5 cm (3″).
Cast off.

Skirt

With white wool cast on 150 sts.
Knit 6 cm (2¼″).
Next row. K 3 tog all along the row (50 sts).
Knit 1 row.
Next row. K 2 tog all along the row (25 sts).
Cast off.

Making up

Sew seams on the wrong side, rounding off corners of feet into points and rounding corners of the head. Turn inside out and stuff firmly. Finish sewing up. Sew and stuff arms and sew on to shoulders.

Embroider features with fine wool or embroidery silk.

Hair

Cut brown or yellow wool into 20 cm (8″) lengths, lay it across the head from shoulder to shoulder (Fig 20) and fasten down the middle of the head with back-stitch. Spread out to cover the back of the head, draw down in two wings each side of the face and take the ends to the back of the neck. Twist them into a knot and sew them down to the head.

Skirt

Cut three or four lengths of net, tulle or tarlatan 5 cm (2″) wide, place them all together and gather them along one side with double cotton. Gather it up tightly and sew on round the waist. Pull the frills out separately. Sew the seam of the skirt and sew it in place on top of the net skirt.

Sew silver cord in a wavy design round the edge of the skirt, and in zigzags along the bodice, finishing in front with a bow.

Make a small wreath of silver cord and sew on the head like a coronet.

A long-legged circus clown
(see p 86)

He is one with very large, long boots whose clothes are all too big for him.

You will need:

Approx 1½ 50-gramme balls (2 oz) of
black wool; approx ½ 50-gramme (1 oz) ball
each of rust colour, jade, white, yellow
and orange 4 ply or double knitting wool;
three No 10 knitting pins; scraps of red
and black felt for features;
kapok for stuffing.

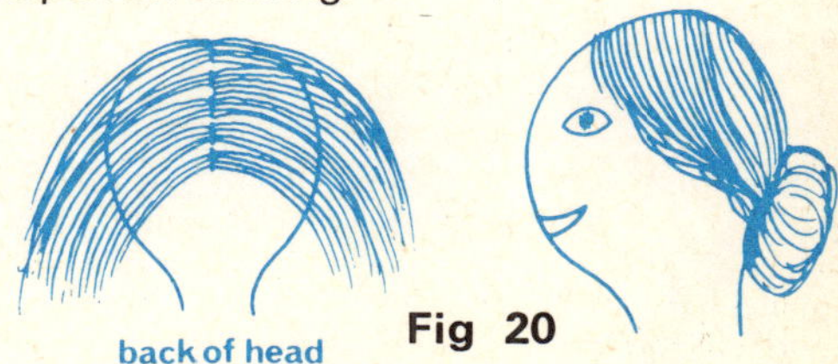

Fig 20

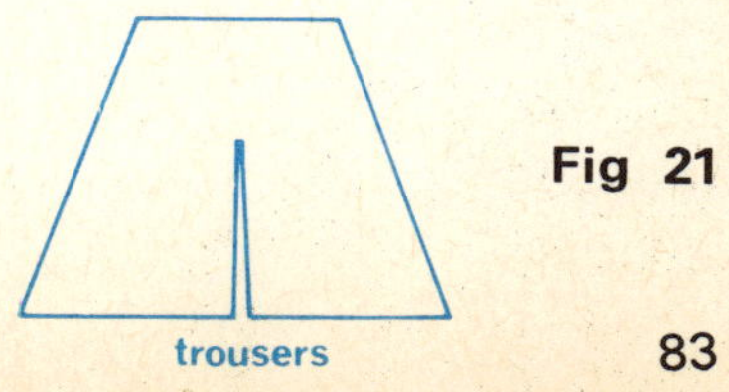

Fig 21

Boots

With black wool cast on 8 stitches.

Knit 5 rows.

Increase each end of the next and every sixth row till there are 16 sts.

Decrease each end of every sixth row till 10 sts are left.

Knit on these 10 sts till work measures 21.5 cm (8½″).

Break off wool and leave sts on needle.

Knit a second leg to match and put both sets of sts on to one needle (20 sts).

Knit 4 cm (1½″) in black wool.

Change to orange and yellow wool.

Knit 2 rows each in orange and yellow wool starting with orange, for 7.5 cm (3″).

Change to white wool.

Knit 5 cm (2″) for the face.

Knit 7.5 cm (3″) in black wool.

Change to orange and yellow wool.

Knit 7.5 (3″), reversing the stripes from those on the front and finishing with orange.

Knit 4 cm (1½″) in black wool and divide for legs.

Knit 11 cm (4½″) on first 10 sts.

Next row. Increase at each end of the next and every sixth row till there are 16 sts.

Decrease each end of every sixth row till 8 sts remain.

Knit 5 rows.

Cast off.

Rejoin wool to other 10 sts and complete it to match the first leg.

Cast off.

Arms

With white wool cast on 16 sts and knit 2.5 cm (1″).

Change to orange and yellow wool and knit in stripes for 6.5 cm (2½″).

Cast off.

Trousers

With rust-coloured wool cast on 25 sts.

Knit 4 rows.

Knit 2 tog at the beginning of the next and every 4th row till 14 sts remain.

Knit 1 row.

Break off wool and leave sts on needle.

Knit a second trouser leg to match.

Put both sets of stitches on to one needle with the straight edges together and the slanting edges on the outside.

Knit on these 28 sts for 4 cm (1½″).

Cast off.

Knit a matching piece for the back of the trousers (Fig 21).

Coat back

Cast on 36 sts in jade wool.

Knit 14 rows.

Join on black wool.

Knit 2 rows.

Break off black wool.

Repeat these 16 rows once.

Knit 10 rows in jade wool, finishing on the wrong side.

Cast off 4 sts at the beginning of the next 2 rows for the armhole and cast off 2 sts at the beginning of the following 2 rows (6 each side).

Join black wool.

Knit 2 rows.

Knit 13 rows in jade wool.

Cast off.

Coat—left front

Cast on 20 sts in jade wool.

Knit 14 rows.

Join black wool.

Knit 2 rows.

Repeat these 16 rows once.

Knit 10 rows of jade wool.

Cast off 4 sts at the beginning of the next row.

Knit 1 row.

Cast off 2 sts at the beginning of the following row.

Knit 1 row.

Knit 2 rows in black wool.

Knit 13 rows in jade wool.

Cast off.

Coat—right front

Knit as for left front as far as the armhole, but knit 11 rows instead of 10.

Next row (wrong side). Cast off 4 sts, knit 1 row.

Cast off 2 sts at the beginning of the following row.

Knit 2 rows in black wool.

Knit 13 rows in jade wool.

Cast off.

Mark along the back of the jacket edge in quarters and, with black wool, work stem stitch or back-stitch from neck to hem of the jacket to give a plaid design.

Work a row right down the centre of the fronts.

Hat brim

With black wool cast on 72 sts.

Knit 2 rows.

Next row. *K 2, k 2 tog.* Repeat * to * to the end of the row (36 sts).

Cast off.

Making up

Sew all seams on the wrong side, leaving one side open for stuffing. Turn inside out, stuff firmly and sew up the opening. Sew and stuff arms and sew on at the shoulder.

Pinch up a tuck over each instep and sew firmly to give some shape to the feet.

Sew the trousers seams. Make a chain or cord with wool and fasten it to the trousers top, over the shoulder and down to the back for a single brace.

Join the side and shoulder seams of the coat and fasten it in front with a big black felt bow. Coat and trousers are purposely made too big for him.

Features

Cut two ovals in black felt for eyes. Work several straight stitches in blue in the ovals, slightly to the sides, and sew them in place with small stitches.

Cut a kidney-shaped large oval in red felt, trim away a slit in the middle and stitch on for his mouth.

A pear-shaped piece of red felt makes a nose for him.

Hat

Join up the seam of the hat brim and sew it on round the top of the head.

With orange wool make a wispy fringe of hair sticking out over the hat brim.

A Pearly King and Queen

They are resplendent in their best clothes, covered with pearl buttons.

The body for each is knitted in two parts – a front and a back.

Pearly King

You will need:

Approx 1½ 50-gramme balls (2 oz) black, approx ½ 50-gramme ball (1 oz) of flesh pink and brown 4 ply or double knitting wool; about 150 small pearl buttons; a little fine red wool for a neckerchief; four No 10 knitting pins; kapok for stuffing.

Legs

Cast on 10 stitches in black wool.

Knit 5 cm (2").

Break off wool and leave sts on needle.

Bell bottoms

Cast on 16 sts in black wool.

Knit 4 rows.

Knit 2 tog at each end of the next and every 4th row till 10 sts are left.

Knit 1 row.

Knit it on to the legs as follows: Place the needle with the bell bottom in front of the needle with the leg sts and knit tog 1 stitch from each needle to the end (10 sts).

Continue knitting till leg measures 11 cm (4½") from the beginning.

Break off wool and leave sts on needle.

Knit a second leg to match and put both sets of sts on to one needle (20 sts).

Knit 11 cm (4½").

Change to pink wool.

Knit 5 cm (2").

Knit 1.25 cm (½") in black wool.

Cast off.

For the back – repeat all the above directions to the end of the body knitting.

Change to brown wool.

Knit 5 cm (2").

Knit 1.25 cm (½") in black wool. Cast off.

Arms

Cast on 16 sts in pink wool.
Knit 1.25 cm (½'').
Change to black wool.
Knit 6.5 cm (2½'').
Cast off.

Coat bottom

Knit the two big patch pockets first.
Cast on 16 sts in black wool.
Knit 4 cm (1½'').
Break off wool and leave.
Cast on 36 sts in black wool.
Knit 5 cm (2'').

Next row. Knit 10, now knit pocket flap on by placing it in front of the coat and knitting tog 1 stitch from each needle till all the pocket sts are used, then knit the remaining 10 sts of the coat (36 sts).

Knit until the work measures 6 cm (2¼'') from the beginning.

Next row. * K 1, k 2 tog. * Repeat * to * to end of row (24 sts).

Cast off.

Knit a second one to match.

Cap brim

Cast on 16 sts in black wool.
Knit 1 row.
Next row. K 14, turn.
K 12, turn.
Continue, knitting 2 sts less in each row till 2 sts are left.
Knit to end of row.
Cast off.

Neckerchief

Cast on 2 sts.
Knit 2 rows.
Increase in next and every 5th row till there are 5 sts.
Knit till work measures 11 cm (4½'') from the beginning.
Decrease in every 5th row till 2 sts remain.
Knit 4 rows.
Cast off.

Making up

Sew all seams from the wrong side, leaving one side open for stuffing and rounding off the corners of head and feet.

Turn inside out and sew on the pearl buttons in a pattern before doing any stuffing. He has ten sewn across the chest in a pattern of two fives (Fig 22), a big one just above them, and six each side up to the shoulders like lapels. Sew them round three sides of the pocket flaps and a double row down what will be the front of the pieces for the coat bottom.

Sew twelve more in the fives pattern on the waist and the rest in two pyramid shapes on the bell bottoms, starting with five on the bottom and decreasing to one as they go up the leg.

Keep twelve to sew in smaller pyramids on the arms, and about 30 of the smallest to sew on the cap.

Stuff the body firmly and sew up the opening. Sew and stuff arms and sew in place.

Features

Embroider these in wool or silk.

Sew on the coat bottoms to overlap at front and back with buttoned piece in the front.

Sew up bell-bottom seams.

Sew cap brim on to the first row of black knitting over the face.

Tie his red neckerchief round his neck with the two ends in front.

Pearly Queen

You will need:

Approx 1½ 50-gramme balls (2 oz) of black wool, approx ½ 50-gramme ball (1 oz) of flesh pink wool (you will probably have enough left over from the pearly king); some fine pink wool or silk for her scarf; and some brown for her hair; some small white feathers; about 80 small pearl buttons; four No 10 knitting pins; kapok for stuffing.

Legs

Cast on 10 stitches in black wool.
Knit 11 cm (4½'').
Break off wool and leave sts on needle.
Knit a second leg to match.
Put both sets of stitches on to one needle and knit 4 cm (1½'') on these 20 sts.
Break off wool and leave.

Skirt

With black wool cast on 36 sts.
Knit 7.5 cm (3'').
Next row. K 2, k 2 tog,* k 4, k 2 tog.* Repeat * to * 4 times, k 2 (30 sts).
Knit 2.5 cm (1'') without decreasing.
Next row. K 1, k 2 tog,* k 3, k 2 tog.* Repeat * to * 4 times. K 2 (24 sts).
Knit 2.5 cm (1'').

Next row. K 2, k 2 tog, * k 4, k 2 tog.* Repeat * to * twice, k 2 (20 sts).

Knit 1.25 cm (½").

Join the skirt on to the body in the same way as the bell bottoms on to the trousers for the pearly king.

Knit in black wool on these 20 sts for 7.5 cm (3").

Change to flesh pink wool.

Knit 5 cm (2").

Knit 1.25 cm (½") in brown wool.

Cast off.

For the back – repeat the above directions to the end of the body knitting.

Change to brown wool and knit 6.5 cm (2½").

Cast off.

Arms

Cast on 16 sts in pink wool.

Knit 1.25 cm (½").

Knit 6.5 cm (2½") in black wool.

Cast off.

Bottom of coat

Cast on 60 sts in black wool.

Knit 5 cm (2").

Next row. * K 1, k 2 tog.* Repeat * to * to end of row (40 sts).

Cast off.

Hat brim and crown

Cast on 80 sts in black wool.

Knit 3 rows.

Next row.* K 2, k 2 tog.* Repeat * to * to end of row (60 sts).

Knit 3 rows.

Next row.* K 1, k 2 tog. * Repeat * to * to end of row (40 sts).

Knit 3 rows.

Next row. K 3, k 2 tog,* k 6, k 2 tog.* Repeat * to * 3 times, k 3 (35 sts).

Knit 3 rows.

Next row. K 3, k 2 tog,* k 5, k 2 tog.* Repeat * to * 3 times, k 2 (30 sts).

Knit 3 rows.

Next row. K 2, k 2 tog,* k 4, k 2 tog.* Repeat * to * 3 times, k 2 (25 sts).

Knit 3 rows.

Next row. K 2, k 2 tog, * k 3, k 2 tog.* Repeat * to * 3 times, k 1 (20 sts).

Knit 3 rows.

Next row. K 1, k 2 tog, * k 2, k 2 tog.* Repeat * to * 3 times, k 1 (15 sts).

Knit 1 row.

Next row * K 1, k 2 tog. * Repeat * to * to end (10 sts).

Knit 1 row.

Next row. K 2 tog five times (5 sts).

Run a thread through the 5 sts and fasten off.

Neckerchief

With pink wool cast on 2 sts.

Knit 5 rows.

Increase in the first stitch in the next and every 6th row till there are 13 sts.

Knit 5 rows.

Decrease at the beginning of the next and every 6th row till 2 sts are left.

Cast off.

Making up

Oversew seams on the wrong side, leaving one side open for stuffing and rounding off corners for head and feet. Turn inside out and stuff firmly. Sew side seams of skirt on wrong sides. Sew the bottom of the coat on at the waistline.

Sew pearl buttons on bodice and skirt and bottom of coat in pattern. Sew a pyramid of them on the arms, and some on the back also.

Sew the hat seam and decorate the brim with small feathers. These can be curled slightly by pulling the feather smartly between the thumb and the open blade of a pair of scissors.

Embroider the features with wool or silk. Twist strands of wool into a chignon and sew to head at the back.

Attach the hat to the head with invisible stitches.

Tie scarf round her neck.

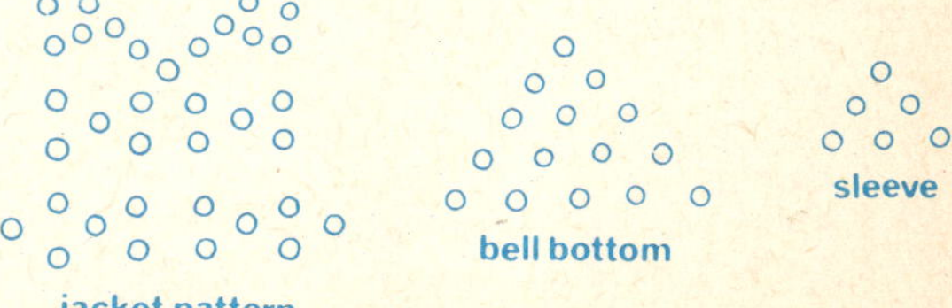

Fig 22

Pierrot

(see p 84)

You will need:

Approx 2 50-gramme balls (3 oz) of white 4 ply or double knitting wool; small quantities of red, orange, green, black wool; three No 10 knitting pins; small piece of red felt; kapok for stuffing.

Cast on 10 stitches in black wool.
Knit 4 cm (1½″).
Change to white wool.
Knit 7.5 cm (3″).
Break off wool and leave sts on needle.
Knit a second leg and put both on to one needle (20 sts).
Knit 16.5 cm (6½″) in white wool.
Knit 7.5 cm (3″) in black wool.
Knit 16.5 cm (6½″) in white wool.
Divide for legs and knit them to match the front ones.

Arms

Cast on 16 sts in white wool.
Knit 7.5 cm (3″).
Cast off.

Making up

Sew seams on the wrong side, leaving an opening for stuffing and rounding off the corners of head and feet. Turn inside out and stuff. Finish sewing up. Sew and stuff arms and sew on at the shoulders.

Cut a long oval in red felt, cut a slit in the middle and sew in place for the mouth.

Embroider two big crosses in black chain stitch for the eyes.

Nose

Cast on 4 sts of red wool.
Knit 1 row.
Increase at the beginning and end of the next row.
Knit 1 row.
Repeat the last 2 rows (8 sts).
Knit 4 rows.
Decrease at the beginning and end of the next row.
Knit 1 row.
Repeat these 2 rows (4 sts).
Cast off.

Run a gathering thread round the edge of the knitting, put a hard ball of stuffing in the middle, draw it up tightly into a ball and sew it in the centre of the face.

Dress

Front.
Cast on 10 sts in white wool.
Knit 1 row.
In the next row increase twice in every stitch by knitting into the front, the back and then the front again (30 sts).
Knit 7 cm (2¾″) on these sts.
Break off the wool and leave.
Knit a second leg to match and put both sets of stitches on to 1 needle (60 sts).
Knit 2.5 cm (1″).
Next row. K 5, k 2 tog, * k 10, k 2 tog.* Repeat * to * 3 times, k 5 (55 sts).
Knit 2.5 cm (1″), including decrease row.
Next row. K 4, k 2 tog, * k 9, k 2 tog.* Repeat * to * 3 times (50 sts).
Knit 2.5 cm (1″).
Next row. K 4, k 2 tog, * k 8, k 2 tog.* Repeat * to * 3 times (45 sts).
Knit 2.5 cm (1″).
Next row. K 3, k 2 tog, * k 7, k 2 tog.* Repeat * to * 3 times (40 sts).
Knit 2.5 cm (1″).
Next row. K 3, k 2 tog, * k 6, k 2 tog.* Repeat * to * 3 times (35 sts).
Knit 2.5 cm (1″).
Next row. K 3, k 2 tog, * k 5, k 2 tog.* Repeat * to * 3 times (30 sts).
Knit on without further decreasing until work measures 23 cm (9″) from the beginning.
Next row. * K 1, k 2 tog.* Repeat * to * to end of row (20 sts).
Cast off.
Knit a second piece for the back of the dress.

Neck and ankle ruffles

With orange wool cast on 60 sts.
Knit 1 row.
Change to white wool.
Knit 4 rows.
Change to green wool.
Knit 2 rows.
Change to white wool.
Knit 2 rows.
Next row. Slip 1, k 2 tog, pass slipped stitch over. Repeat this to the end of the row (20 sts).
Cast off.
Knit two more ruffles for the ankles.

Sleeve ruffles

With orange wool cast on 48 sts.
Knit 1 row.
Break off wool.
Change to white wool.
Knit 4 rows.
Change to green wool.
Knit 2 rows.
Change to white wool.
Knit 2 rows.
Next row. Slip 1, knit 2 tog, pass slipped stitch over. Repeat this to the end of the row (16 sts).
Cast off.
Knit a second one to match.

Hat

With white wool cast on 48 sts.
Knit 4 cm (1½").
Next row. *K 6, k 2 tog.* Repeat * to * to end of the row (42 sts).
Knit 3 rows.
Next row. *K 5, k 2 tog.* Repeat * to * to end of row (36 sts).
Knit 3 rows.
Next row. *K 4, k 2 tog.* Repeat * to * to end of row (30 sts).
Knit 3 rows.
Next row. *K 3, k 2 tog.* Repeat * to * to end of row (24 sts).
Knit 3 rows.
Next row. *K 2, k 2 tog.* Repeat * to * to end of next row (18 sts).
Knit 3 rows.
Next row. *K 1, k 2 tog.* Repeat * to * to end of row (12 sts).
Knit 3 rows.
Next row. Knit 2 tog all along the row (6 sts).
Knit 3 rows.
Next row. K 2 tog 3 times (3 sts).
Next row. Slip 1, knit 1, pass slipped stitch over.
Cast off.

Bobbles

Cut two strips of cardboard 1.25 cm (½") wide. Place them together with a thread of wool between them lengthways (Fig 23). Wind orange wool round them about 50 times. Cut through the wool between the cards and tie very tightly round the middle to form a ball. Trim off the ends to the required size. Make two or three for the hat and three for the dress.

Making up

Sew together the inside leg seams.
Pin the centre of the neck of the dress to the doll's neck, similarly pin the back. Pin the trouser legs together at the ankles. They should be slightly baggy.
Oversew the side seams on the right side. Catch down to the doll at neck and ankles. Join shoulder seams.
Join seams of ruffles and sew them round neck and ankles and the two smaller ones round the wrists.

Sew three bobbles down the front.

Sew seam of hat, turn brim back in a roll (Fig 24) and catch down. Sew on bobbles, stuff lightly to keep shape and stitch to the head through the brim.

Fig 23

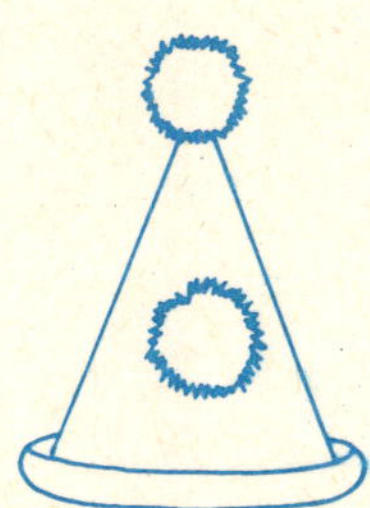

Fig 24

cut away all shaded parts
Fig 1
Fig 2
(actual size)

CHAPTER FOUR

Masks and head-dresses

Masks for all sorts of games and simple dramatization, where elaborate costumes for dressing up are not practicable, can be made from Vilene or tarlatan. Vilene in black and white is made in different thicknesses, and the white can very easily be painted or crayoned. Tarlatan comes in many lovely bright colours, as well as black and white and is best used for masks and head-dresses in two or more thicknesses.

A highwayman's mask

This can be made in either material. Cut a pattern from an oval shape which stretches from ear to ear and is wide enough to cover the top half of the face to the tip of the nose, about 20 cm by 10 cm (8″ by 4″). Cut it into a shallow 'V' above and below the nose. Fold it in half and mark the position of the eyes. Cut out two ovals pointed at each end. Place this pattern on the tarlatan layers and cut it out (Fig 1). With double embroidery silk in a contrasting colour, stitch the layers together with running stitch round the outside edges, and round the eye edges. Fasten strands of silk at each side to tie at the back of the head or sew on elastic to hold it firmly on the head.

A Red Indian head-dress

You will need:

A piece of tarlatan for a band, and several smaller pieces in different colours; some embroidery silks.

Cut a piece of coloured tarlatan 20 cm (8″) wide and long enough to fit round your head and to overlap a little. Draw a leaf or feather shape about 15 cm (6″) long (Fig 2) and cut out about 30 cm (12″) in double tarlatan in several colours.

Fasten the layers of each feather shape together with running stitch. Fold the long piece of tarlatan in half and arrange the feathers along one edge. Fold the strip in half again to cover the end of the feathers so that they are enclosed in the band (Fig 3). Sew them in place with running stitch and work some simple designs on the band. Sew a piece of Velcro at each end of the band and it can then be made to fit your head comfortably.

Fig 3

Fig 4

Fig 5

A simple crown

Make this a double strip of tarlatan. Cut one edge into points or leaf shapes and fasten the double layers together with running stitch. Sequins and fine metal-thread can be used to decorate it. Sew on Velcro at each end to fasten it.

The points are shown in Fig 4, the leaf shapes in Fig 5.

A pirate's hat

You will need:

Black tarlatan and a little white Vilene or felt.

Draw the shape of the hat on paper, then cut this out to use as a pattern.

Cut out:

the hat in double tarlatan for back and front (Fig 6);

the skull and crossbones (Fig 7) for the front in white Vilene and stick on the front with a clear adhesive.

Sew the two hat pieces together with running stitch as indicated in Fig 6 but leave a big enough opening to fit your head.

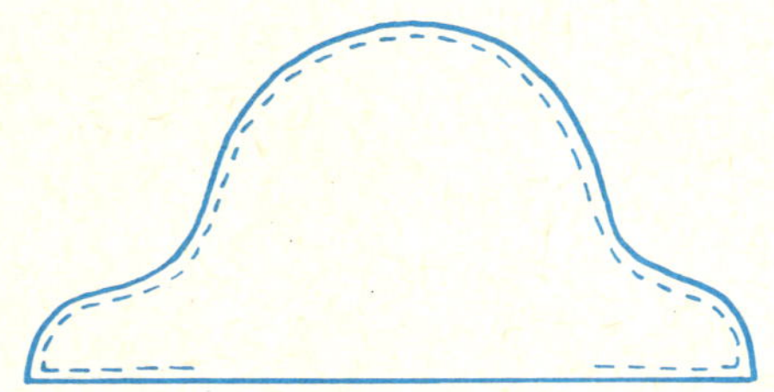

Fig 6

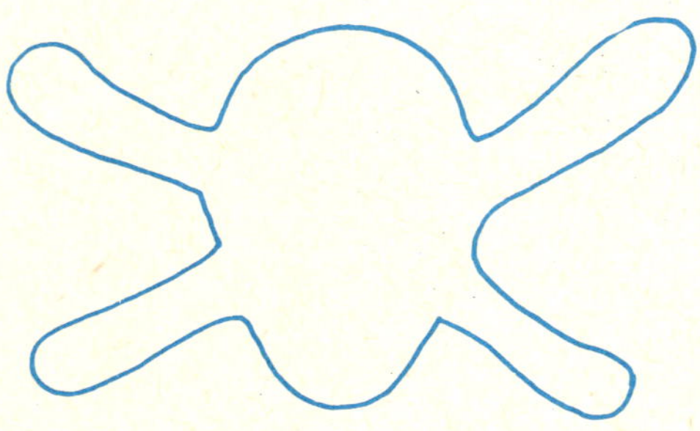

Fig 7
(actual size)

A cat mask

You will need:

Vilene; five black pipe cleaners; green sequins; elastic.

On paper draw a circle big enough to cover your face. Shape the bottom into a pointed chin by cutting the circle away at each side. Add pointed ears at the top (Fig 8). Pin this shape on to the black Vilene and cut it out.

Coil up one of the pipe cleaners and stick it in the centre of the face with a clear adhesive. Fold the pipe cleaners in half and stick down the folded ends each side of the nose for whiskers (Fig 9).

Cut two oval eye shapes, slanting in to the nose. Place a piece of green tarlatan behind the face and mark the outline of the eyes lightly with pencil. Stick a ring of green sequins in each eye shape with clear adhesive (Fig 10), then stick the tarlatan in position behind the face so that the sequinned eyes fill the eyeholes in the mask (Fig 11). Sew an end of thin elastic each side of the mask to fit round the head.

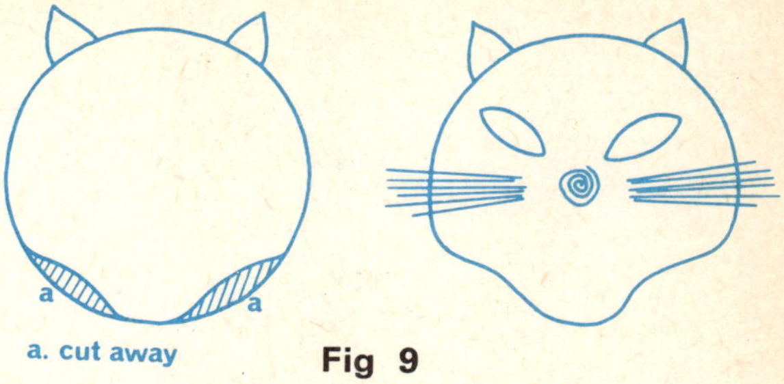

a a

a. cut away

Fig 9

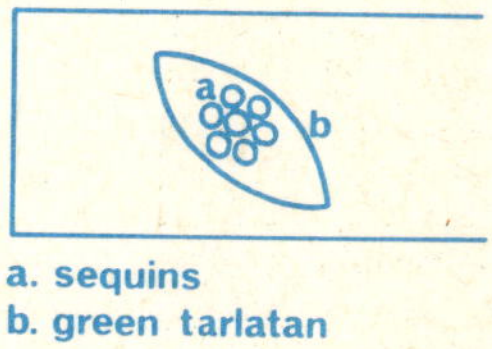

a b

a. sequins
b. green tarlatan

Fig 10

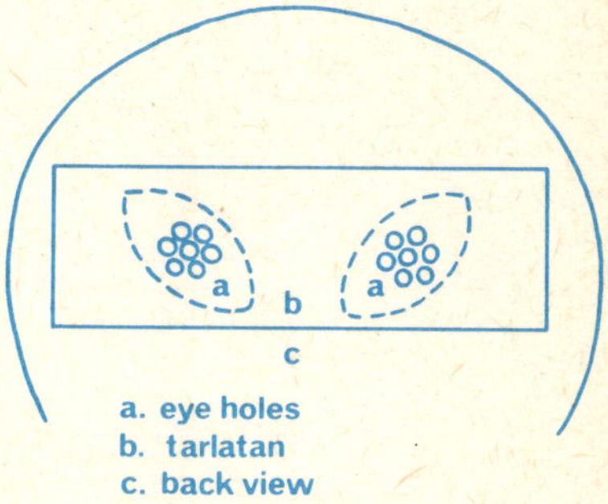

a b a
c

a. eye holes
b. tarlatan
c. back view

Fig 11

Fig 8

A guardsman mask

You will need:

Black and white Vilene; pink tarlatan.

Cut out:

the shape of face and bearskin in one piece of white Vilene (Fig 14);

a separate bearskin shape in black Vilene, using the top part of the pattern as a guide;

ovals for the eyes and a crescent-shaped mouth;

a face shape in pink tarlatan;

the moustache (Fig 15) and crescent-shaped eyebrows in black Vilene.

Stick these in place with a clear adhesive.

The mouth and red cheeks can be cut out of a scrap of red tarlatan and stuck on, or can be drawn in with a red felt-tip pen.

Fig 12

Fig 13

a. pink felt
b. single chain stitch

A white rabbit mask

For the rabbit you will need:

White Vilene; some scraps of pink felt.

Cut out:

the face from an oval shape in double white Vilene, slightly pointed at the chin and with two long ears added at the top (Fig 12);

nose shape in pink felt and sew it on in the centre of the face;

the oval-shaped eyes above the nose and slanting inwards.

Stick a rectangle of pink tarlatan behind the eye holes with clear adhesive. With pink embroidery silk work a mouth shape as in Fig 13 and some straight stitches each side for whiskers. Sew an end of elastic each side at the back to fit the head.

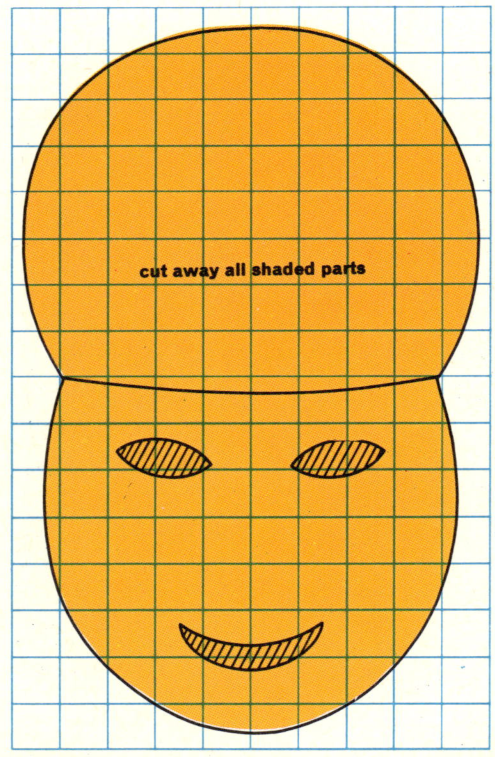

Fig 14

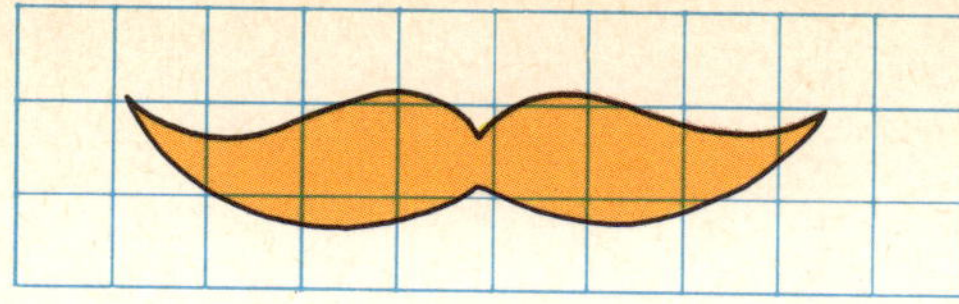

Fig 15

Over the whole white Vilene face, place the pink tarlatan face and stick it down round the edge.

Place the black Vilene bearskin in position and stick it down round the edge. Sew on an elastic at the sides to fit round the head.

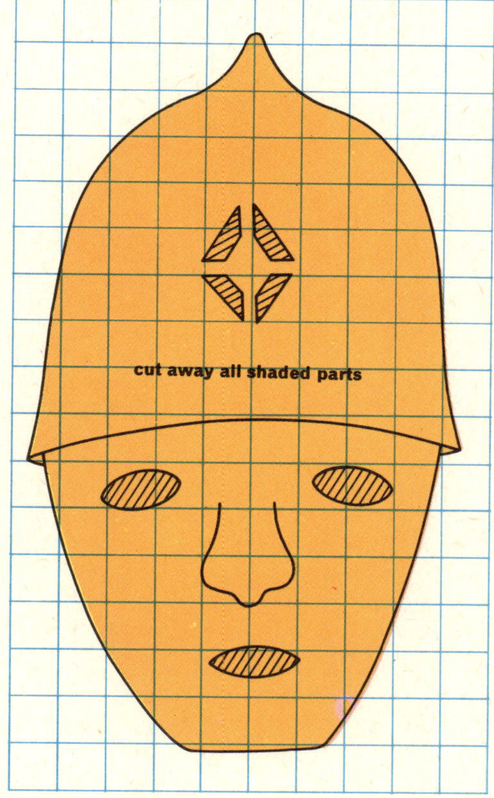

Fig 16

A policeman mask

You will need:

Thick white Vilene; royal blue tarlatan; pink tarlatan.

Cut out the face and helmet in one piece in white Vilene. The helmet is six layers of royal blue tarlatan, cut to shape from the top part of the pattern (Fig 16). Draw the motif shape

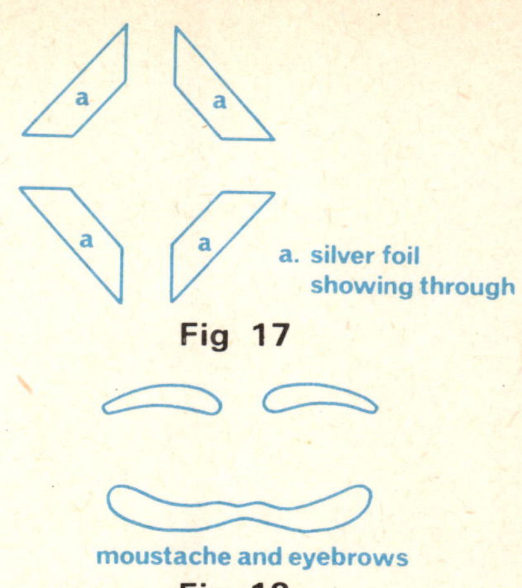

Fig 17

Fig 18

on the helmet with a white pencil and cut through all the layers of tarlatan with a sharp penknife on a hard surface. Paste a square of silver paper behind the cut-out motif so that it shines through on the right side (Fig 17).

Cut the eye holes—rounded ovals—and a crescent-shaped mouth. Cut round the outline of the nose.

Curly moustache and eyebrow crescents are cut from black Vilene or similar material, and stuck in place with clear adhesive (Fig 18).

Cheeks and mouth can be coloured with a red felt-tip pen. Cover the face with the pink tarlatan face and stick it in place round the edge.

Fit the helmet in place and oversew it round the edge and across the head with matching cotton. Sew elastic at the sides to fit round the back of the head.

A pirate mask

You will need:

Thick white Vilene; black Vilene; a felt-tip pen.

Again the hat and face are cut out in one piece in white Vilene. If the Vilene is not very thick, cut it in double thickness (Fig 19).

Cut out:

the hat shape in black Vilene, using the hat shape on the pattern as a guide;

ovals for the eyes;

jagged-edged eyebrows;

a curved mouth;

the centre of the ear ring.

Cut round the outline of the nose.

Colour the face brownish-pink with felt-tip pens, and draw in the mouth in red and the eyebrows and beard in black.

Cut a crescent-shaped moustache in black Vilene and stick it in place. Cut a ring in gold paper to fit the ear ring and stick it over the Vilene ring.

Place the hat in position and oversew all round the edges and across the forehead (see Figs 6 and 7 earlier).

Draw the skull and crossbones in white pencil and cut through black and white layers all together. Sew on a narrow elastic to fit the head.

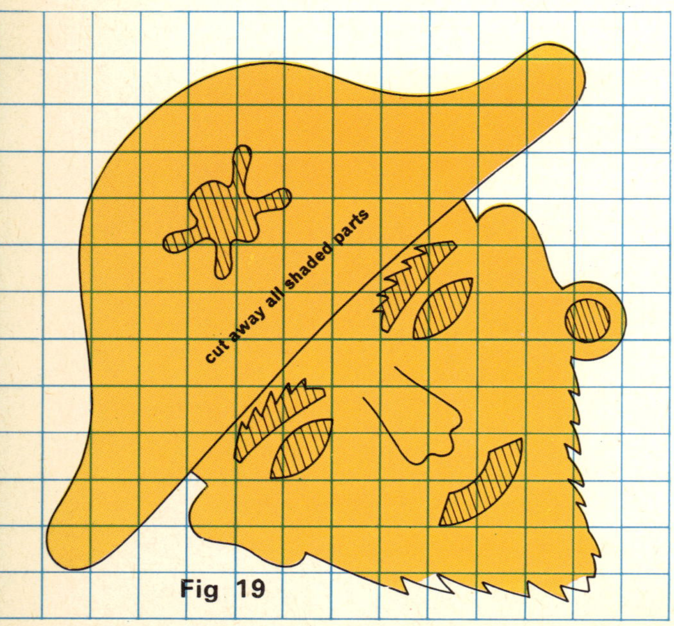

Fig 19

Fig 20

A clown mask

You will need:

Thick white Vilene; red and yellow tarlatan; coloured felt-tip pens.

Cut out:

the hat, face and flower in one piece in white Vilene, in double thickness if the Vilene is not thick enough (Fig 20);

the hat shape in four layers of red tarlatan;

the flower in four layers of yellow tarlatan.

The nose and eyes are big circles.

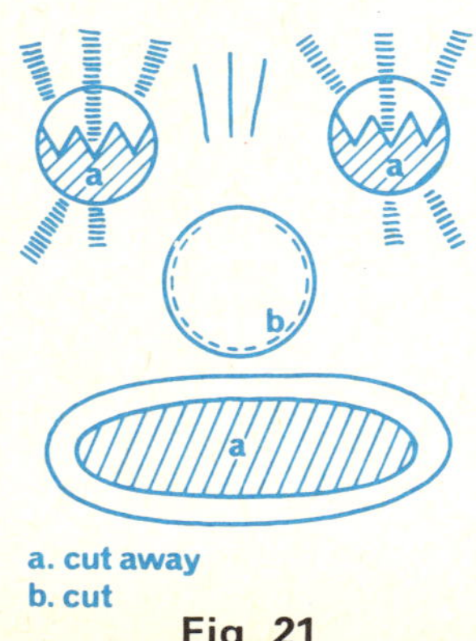

Fig 21

Fig 22

Cut round the bottom half of the eyes and cut the piece out in points for eye lashes (Fig 21).

Colour the nose red with a felt-tip pen and cut round it, leaving a small piece at the top as a hinge.

Cut out the oval mouth and colour all round it with a red felt-tip pen.

Draw face decorations on eyes, cheeks and forehead with felt-tip pens.

Sew a pipe cleaner on the flower stem, place over it the yellow tarlatan shape and oversew all round the edges (Fig 22).

Place the hat in position and sew round the edges and over the forehead. Sew on a narrow elastic to fit the head.

Fig 23

A wolf mask

You will need:

Thick white Vilene; brown and black felt-tip pens.

Cut out:

the whole shape, face and ears, in white Vilene, double thickness if necessary (Fig 23);

the eyes and the mouth curve with jagged teeth at the bottom.

Cut all round the outline of the snout.

Colour all over with black and brown felt-tip pens to simulate fur.

Sew on elastic to fit. To make the ears stand up, the top half of the head and ears can be reinforced with an extra piece of Vilene, cut to shape and stuck on at the back.

Masks for a play — a princess, a witch and a frog prince

The princess

You will need:

White Vilene; gold paper; felt-tip pens.

Cut out:

the face and crown in one piece in thick white Vilene (Fig 24);

two rounded ovals for eyes and a curved mouth.

Cut round the outline of the nose.

Colour the face faintly pink with a pink felt-tip pen, and colour the mouth and cheeks with a red one. Draw in the eyebrows, lashes and hair with a black felt-tip pen.

Trace a gold paper crown from the template and stick it on over the Vilene one. Sew on elastic.

cut away all shaded parts

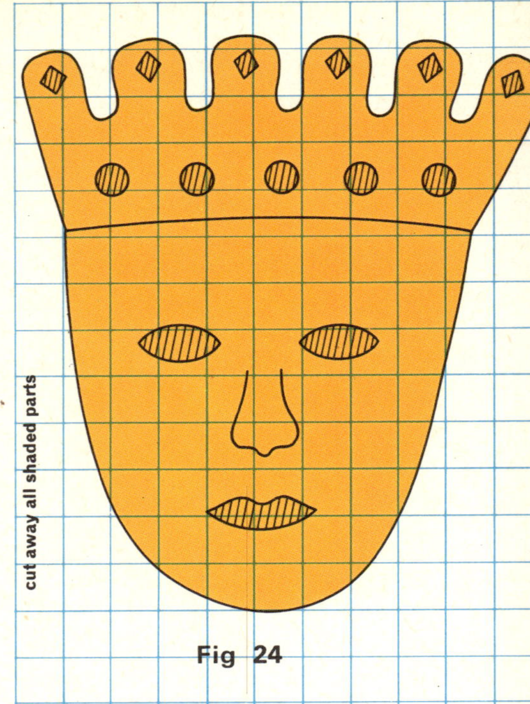

Fig 24

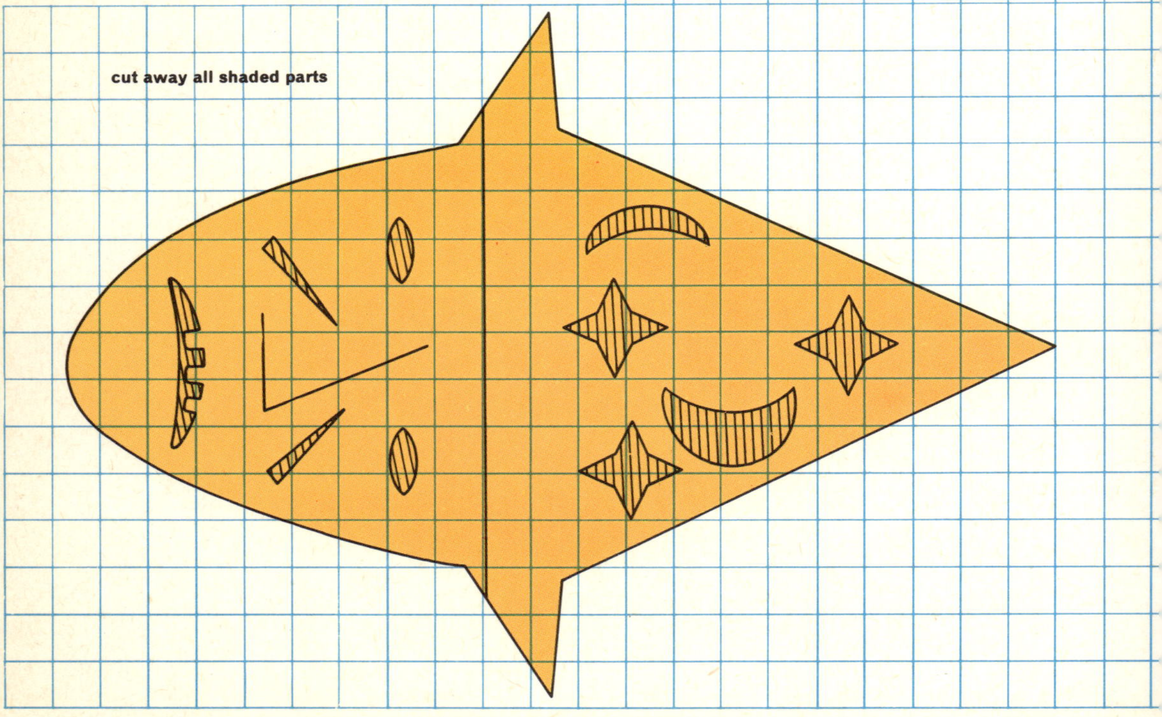

cut away all shaded parts

Fig 25

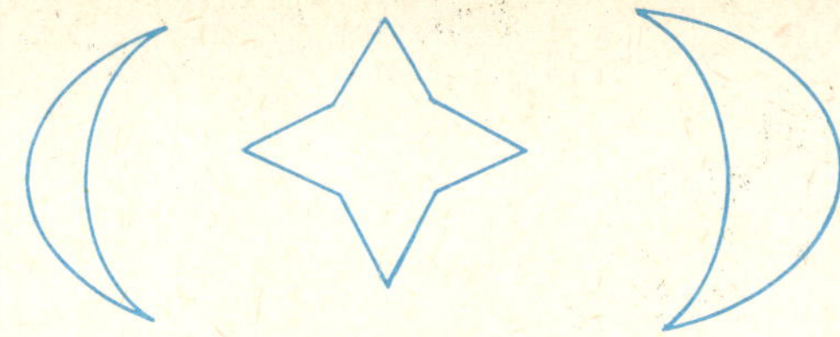

Fig 26

The witch

You will need:

Thick white Vilene; black Vilene; silver paper; a little red and green foil; some felt-tip pens.

Cut out:

the face and hat in white Vilene (Fig 25) and a separate hat in black Vilene;

the crescents and stars from the black Vilene hat (Fig 26); stick silver paper behind the black Vilene, to shine through to the front.

Cut small, slit-like ovals for the eyes and over them stick big triangles in red foil with an oval of green foil in the middle. When it is dry, turn it over and cut the eye shapes through the foil.

Cut down one side and along the base of a pointed nose and cut out a turned-down crescent for a mouth.

Colour the face brownish-red with felt-tip pens, colour the mouth red and draw the eyebrows, bad-temper lines and whiskery chin in black. Fit the black hat on to the shape and either stick or sew it down round the edges. Sew on narrow elastic.

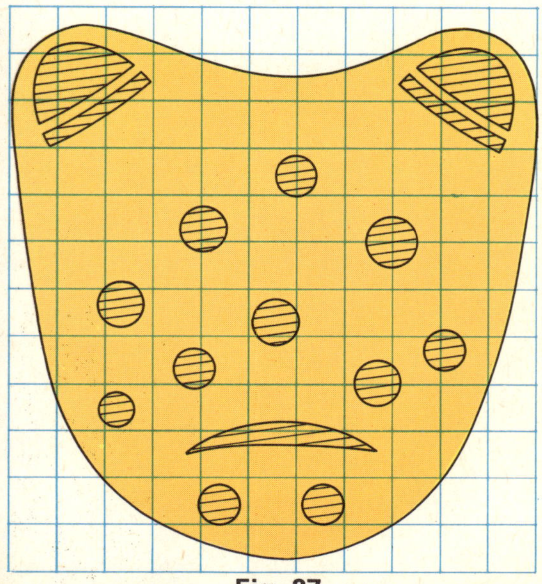

Fig 27

The frog prince

You will need:

White Vilene; green tarlatan; red and green foil.

Cut out:

the shape in thick white Vilene and in double green tarlatan (Fig 27);

the big curved crescent for the mouth, and the spots, cutting out two in convenient places for seeing through.

Stick red foil behind the two frog eyes at the top of the head, and green foil behind some of the spots, but not the peep holes. Cover the front with the green tarlatan face shapes and oversew round the edges. Sew on elastic to fit.

CHAPTER FIVE

Gifts to make

A carry-cot and baby doll

A shoe box was used as the basis for the carry-cot, and the doll baby in it is made from stockinette or woven vest material from an old vest or singlet. The inside of the box has been padded and lined and the outside covered. The one in the picture has white lining with a blue overcheck pattern, whilst the outside reverses this and is blue checked with white. It has a pillow and mattress, sheets, blankets and padded cover, with two handles for easy carrying.

You will need:

The shoe box, which measures 25 cm by 17.5 cm (10″ by 7″); two pieces of material covering it—the outside piece measuring 40.5 cm by 54 cm (16″ by 21½″) and the inside piece 40.5 cm by 48 cm (16″ by 19″); for the mattress and pillow a piece 38 cm (15″) square; two pieces for sheets 38 cm by 23 cm (15″ by 9″) each; two pieces of flannel 19 cm by 28 cm (7½″ by 11″); a pretty piece of nylon 25.5 cm by 28 cm (10″ by 11″) for a cover; a piece 18 cm by 28 cm (7″ by 11″) for a padded quilt; some narrow lace for edging; wadding or thick interlining; sewing cotton; two or three strands of embroidery silks.

The cot

Cover the outside of the box first. Cut off a strip from the larger piece of material measuring 6.5 cm by 40.5 cm (2½″ by 16″) to make the handles, leaving a piece 48 cm by 40.5 cm (19″ by 16″). From each corner of this cut off a square of 11 cm (4½″), leaving a cross-shaped piece (Fig 1).

Use this shape as a pattern, placing it on the wadding and cutting a similar shape from it, the base measuring 25.5 cm by 23 cm (10″ by 11″) but the sides measuring 10 cm (4″) instead of 11 cm (4½″) because it needs to reach only to the top of the box, with no turnings.

Fit the wadding inside the box and fix the top edge in place with masking tape, or stick it with a clear adhesive. Fit the box on to the rectangle in the middle of the cross on the material, turn up the shorter pieces at the ends of the box and pin one side firmly to the wadding on the inside edge. Gently pull the material taut from the other side so that it is firm, and pin that side too. Do not pull it too tightly or it will tear the wadding. The sides of material should lap over on to the long edges (Fig 2). Stick them in place with adhesive, pulling them taut.

Make a single turning on the edges of the long sides and pin it up the corners on to the stuck-down pieces. Lap the material over the top edge of the box and fix it in the same way as the short sides. Sew up the corner seams neatly and catch down the top edges to the wadding, to help in holding it in place.

Cut the 40.5 cm (16″) length of material in half for handles, fold each piece in half lengthways with the right sides inside and seam them. Turn them inside out and press the seams flat. Pin them in position on the inside of the long edges of the box, with the ends at an angle pointing to the bottom corners of the box. Catch down the edges to the wadding and the covering material.

Sew together the edges of the lining material on the wrong side, so that the base measures 25.5 cm by 18 cm (10″ by 7″) (turnings of 1.25 cm (½″) have been allowed for in the pattern). Press the seams flat. Fit the lining into the box, wrong side down, and pin into the corners to keep it in place. Make a turning all round the top edge to come just inside the box, and sew it neatly all round the top, sewing in the handles as well.

If the stitches at the top show, or are not neat enough, couch down a cord or several strands of embroidery silk round the top to cover them. Lay the cord along the join and sew over it through the top edge of the material.

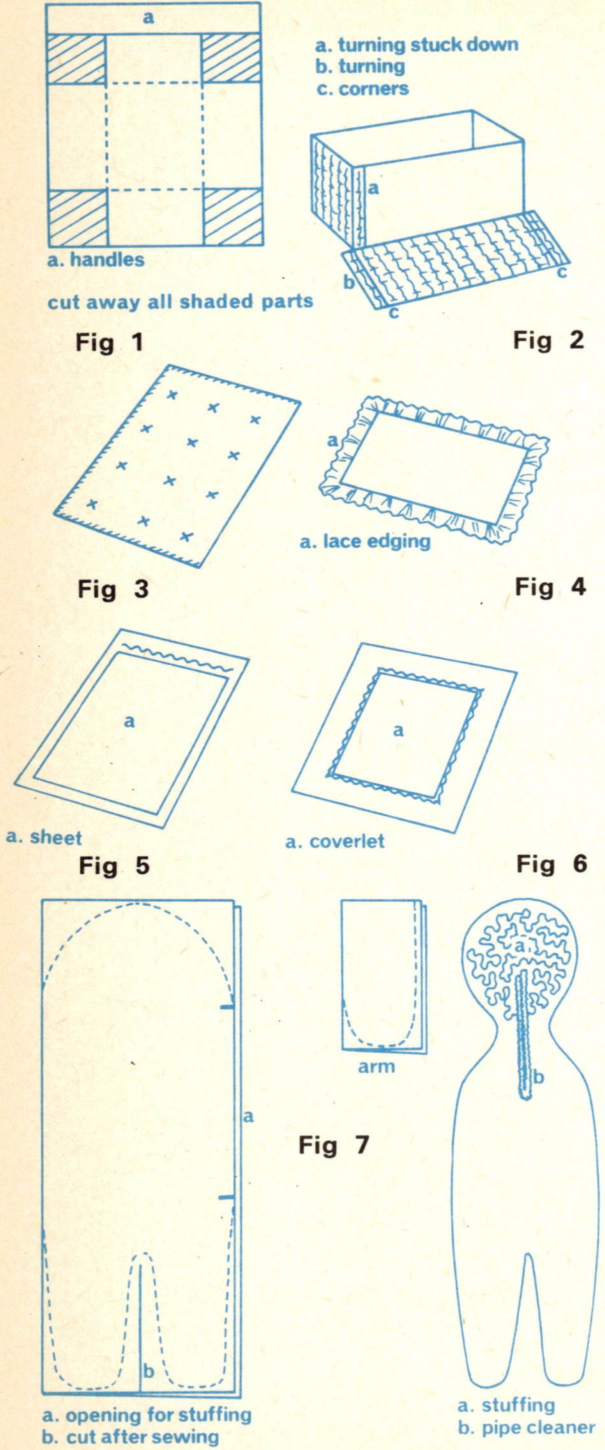

The mattress

Cut a double thickness of wadding to fit the bottom of the box—about 16 cm by 23 cm (6¼″ by 9¼″). From the material for pillow and mattress cut a piece 26 cm (10¼″) wide for the mattress. Fold it in half with right sides inside and seam it together, leaving one side open. Turn inside out. Insert the pad of wadding and sew up the opening.

Sew cross stitches in about twelve places all over the mattress through all the thicknesses to hold the wadding in place (Fig 3).

The pillow

Fold the remaining piece of material in half for the pillow and seam it on the wrong side, leaving one short side open. Turn inside out. Fill it with kapok and sew up the opening. Sew the lace gathered into a frill all round the edge (Fig 4).

The sheets

For the sheets, sew small hems round three sides of the material, making a bigger hem on one of the short sides and embroidering this with threaded or whipped coloured running stitch (Fig 5).

The blankets

Make small hems similarly on all sides of the flannel pieces for the blankets, sewing a row of coloured blanket stitch along the edge of one of the short sides.

The nylon coverlet

This has 2.5 cm (1″) hems on all the sides, sewn down with a decorative running stitch or other embroidery. When finished it should measure about 16.5 cm by 19 cm (6½″ by 7½″) (Fig 6).

The padded quilt

Make a single turning all round the piece of material so that it measures 16 cm by 31.5 cm (6¼″ by 12½″). Cut a square of wadding in double thickness to measure 15 cm (6″). Place it on one-half of the material and fold the other half over it. Tack round the edges, including the wadding edges. Gather up the lace on one edge until it measures 63.5 cm (25″). Pin it evenly all round the edges of the quilt and sew edges and lace together.

The baby doll

You will need:

A piece of stockinette measuring 26.5 cm by 15 cm (10½" by 6") and two pieces 6.5 cm by 7.5 cm (2½" by 3") for arms; (if the material is from a used vest, make sure that no thin, worn parts are included or the doll will not wear well); some kapok or other soft stuffing; a strand each of red, blue, black embroidery silk; some wool for hair; a piece of soft material for a nightgown.

Fold the stockinette in half with the right side inside, lengthways, and back-stitch the shape (Fig 7). Machining it is often not very successful because the material stretches out of shape very easily.

Legs

Cut up between the legs after they have been sewn. Turn it inside out and press out the seams. Stuff the legs and back-stitch across the hips to give some movement and so that the doll can sit. Stuff the head firmly but not hard enough to stretch the fabric and so pull the head out of shape.

Neck

To strengthen the neck and prevent the head drooping, fold a pipe cleaner in half, twist it together and push it into position so that it is in the middle of the neck, half in the head and half in the body (Fig 8). Be careful to pack stuffing all round it to keep it central. Tie a thread tightly round the neck.

Body

Stuff the body firmly, though not quite so firmly as the head, pushing stuffing well up into the neck. Sew up the opening.

Arms

Fold the arm pieces in half lengthways on the wrong side and sew the seam, rounding off the corners for the hands. Turn them inside out, stuff softly and sew them in place across the shoulders.

Features

Embroider a mouth in red silk, two blue spots for eyes surrounded with black back stitch, a few straight stitches for eye lashes and crescents of eyebrows (Fig 9). Sew on wool loops for hair, or lay strands of wool across the head and sew down the middle for a parting, tying it with bows at the sides of the face (Fig 10).

Clothes

Her nightdress is cut from flannelette type material with a small floral pattern, gathered in at the neck, with a lace frill round the neck and hem. Cut it from a length of material 26 cm by 17.7 cm (10½" by 7"). Fold it in half and cut out (Fig 11). Make a narrow hem on the sleeves, neck and bottom. Sew on the lace frills. Run a gathering thread round the neck, draw it up and tie in a bow.

Pop the doll into her cot, cosily between the sheets, and she is ready to go for an outing.

Fig 9

Fig 10

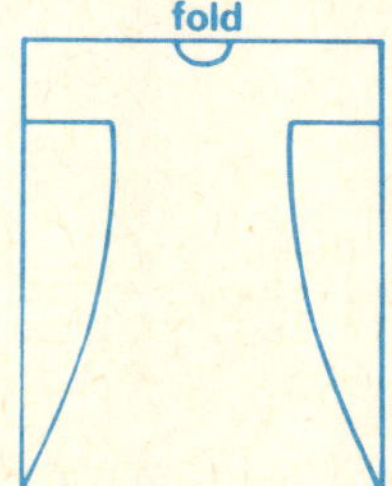

Fig 11

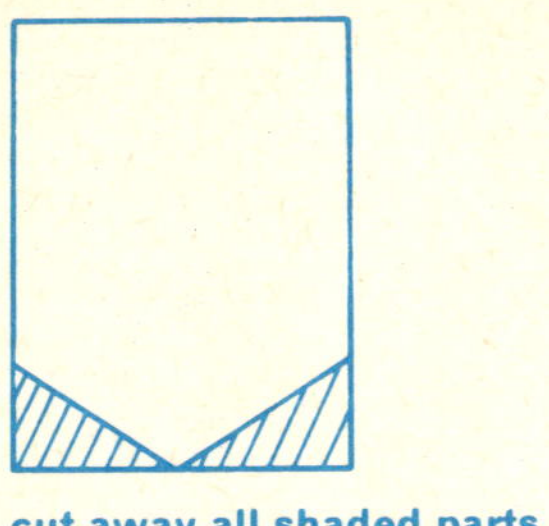

Fig 12

Fig 13

An easy flat money purse

Shaped like an envelope with a triangular flap, the purse is fastened with a looped button, or could have a press stud.

You will need:

A piece of felt 21.5 cm by 11 cm (8½" by 4½"); a piece of lining material 24 cm by 14 cm (9½" by 5½"); some embroidery silks; matching sewing cotton.

Mark 4 cm (1½") up each side at one end of the felt, and mark the middle of the short side of the same end. Cut off these corners to form the front flap (Fig 12). The front of the purse under the flap is 7.5 cm (3") deep, the back is 9 cm (3½") deep and the flap at its widest part in the middle is 5 cm (2").

Embroider the felt before putting in the lining.

The front of this one is embroidered 1.25 cm (½") inside the edge with pointed buttonhole stitch. This is done by putting the needle *in* the same hole three times, but bringing it out each time a little to the right of the last stitch (Fig 13a).

The flap has a centre heart-shaped design in whipped running stitch, the centre filled with leaves of long single chain stitch and yellow back stitch (Fig 13b).

Each side of it is a curlicue in double whipped running stitch.

The button is made of two small circles of felt sewn together, the top circle embroidered in double buttonhole stitch.

A loop for it is made by sewing a double loop on the end of the flap, long enough to encircle the button and these loops then button-hole stitched.

Cut the corners from one end of the piece of lining, make 1.25 cm (½") turnings all round it, and sew it on to the wrong side of the felt. Fold the purse, sew up the side seams and button the flap.

A folding needlecase

You will need:

Two pieces of contrasting coloured felt; a strand each of red, blue and white thick embroidery cotton; red and white embroidery silk; a piece of flannel.

This shape can quite easily be adapted to use as a purse or a needlecase. The one in the picture (see p 110) is a needlecase made of dark blue felt, and is lined with white felt. The fastening flap is cut in one with the case (Fig 14).

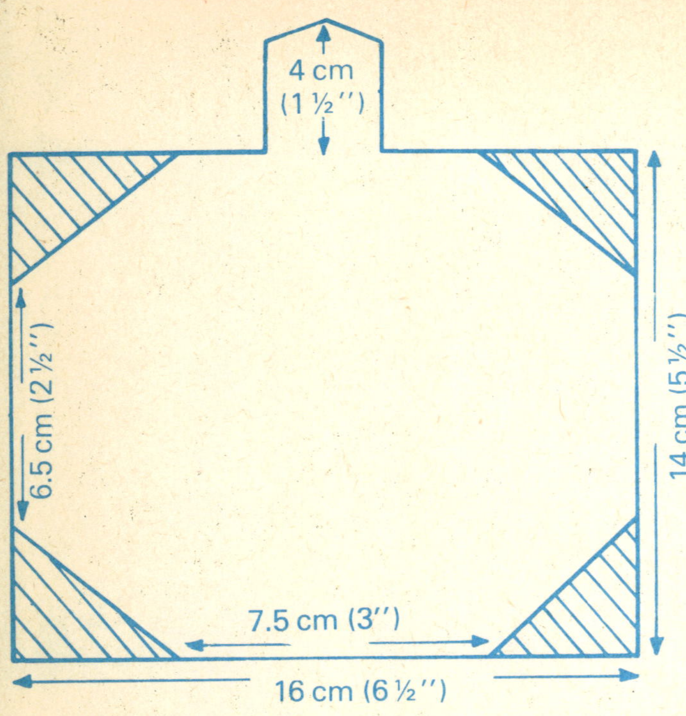

cut away all shaded parts

Fig 14

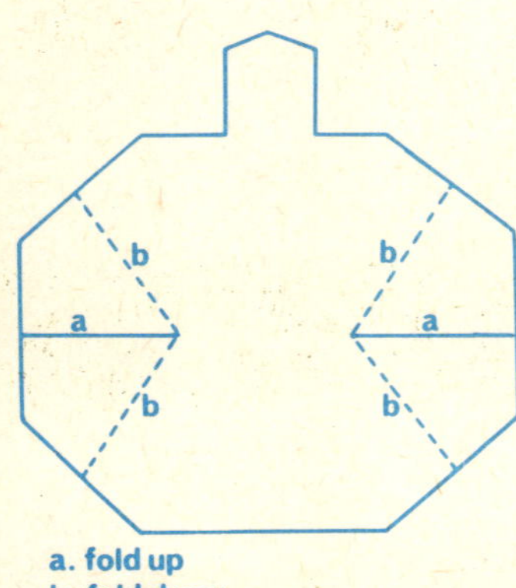

Fig 15

Trace once round the template on each piece of felt, and cut round the pencil lines with pinking shears to give a serrated edge. Two lines of couching are the only decoration on the outside and one line on the inner side.

Couch a line of thick red embroidery cotton close to the edge with white embroidery silk, and inside that a line of thick white cotton couched down with a red thread. Similarly, on the white lining felt couch down a line of thick blue cotton with white thread.

Sew three small rectangles of serrated-edged flannel to the middle of the white felt, the short side nearest to the flap. Place the two felt shapes together with right sides outside and sew them together with invisible stitches, hidden by the couching. Fig 15 will help you in making the folds on each side – the middle ones fold up towards the centre and those each side fold down from the centre. When folded correctly, the corners of the serrated edge should be together. Fasten with a stud.

An embroidered pencil case

This is an easy envelope shape.

You will need:

A single strip of felt measuring
43 cm by 7.5 cm (17″ by 3″); another strip of different-coloured felt for lining to make it stronger also 43 cm by 7.5 cm (17″ by 3″); or a piece of closely woven material 45.5 cm by 10 cm (18″ by 4″) to allow 1.25 cm (½″) turnings all round; red and yellow embroidery silks.

The front is 15 cm (6″) deep and the flap 12.5 cm (5″). A line of whipped running stitch is sewn 6 mm (¼″) in from the edge and all round it.

On the flap, three interlaced circles are outlined in yellow chain stitch, whipped with red on the inner arcs and blanket stitch worked over it on the outer arcs (Fig 16a).

On the front are embroidered two separate circles. The edges are blanket-stitched in yellow which is whipped with red. A cross of red chain stitch from edge to edge of the circle has shorter diagonal lines of chain stitch in between. In their spaces, are single chain (or lazy daisy) stitches in yellow (Fig 16b).

Make 1.25 cm (½″) turnings on the lining and sew it on to the wrong side of the felt.

Turn the front of the case up 15 cm (6'') and oversew the edges. If felt is used for lining, then oversew the two pieces together all round and then sew the side seams.

A case for your recorder

It is a tube of felt, with a circle of felt-covered card at one end and a drawstring at the other.

You will need:

A piece of felt as long as your recorder plus 2.5 cm (1'') and about 12.5 cm (5'') wide; a piece of lining 2.5 cm (1'') longer and 2.5 cm (1'') wider than the felt;
a circle of felt 3 cm (1⅛'') in diameter and the lining 5 cm (2'') in diameter;
a circle of card slightly less than 3 cm (1⅛'') in diameter.

This case is embroidered in two panels running round the case. Two circles of threaded running stitch have an eight-pointed star of straight stitch in the centre, each stitch tipped with a single chain stitch (Fig 17). Two lines of couched thick embroidery cotton each side of the circles complete each panel.

Sew the lining side seams (1.25 cm (½'') turnings are allowed). Make 1.25 cm (½'') turnings at the top and bottom, press the seam flat and lay the lining tube on the wrong side of the felt.

Pin the top and bottom edges of the felt to the lining. Pin the side seam of the felt, taking care to match the embroidery. Oversew the felt seam and sew the lining in place at top and bottom.

Snip nearly 1.25 cm (½'') cuts round the lining circle, turn it in to the centre and place it on the felt circle (Fig 18). Oversew the circles together halfway round, slide in the card circle and complete the oversewing. Oversew this circle to one end of the felt tube.

Sew a row of running stitches with embroidery silk 1.25 cm (½'') from the top edge and a second row 1.25 cm (½'') below it. On the lining cut a small slit between the two rows of running stitches. Oversew all round the slit to make an eyelet hole. Run a cord or ribbon through the two rows of running stitch and draw up the top.

Fig 16

Fig 17

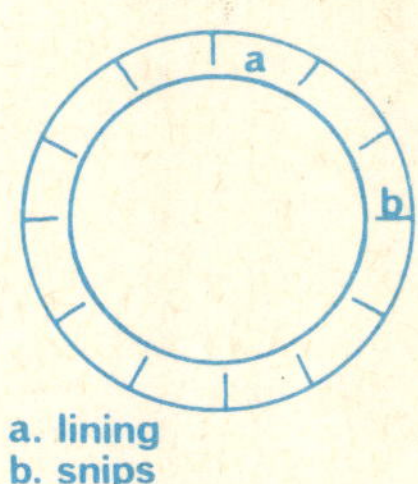

Fig 18

A housewife

This seems a very strange name for a little case which holds pins, needles and cotton, a useful travelling case on holiday when you need to do some quick repairs.

This one is made of dark red felt em-

broidered in black, yellow and turquoise, and is lined with white felt. A cord running through the centre holds the reels of cotton in place.

You will need:

Two pieces of felt 21.5 cm by 9 cm (8½" by 3½"); two circles of felt in each colour 4 cm (1½") diameter; a piece of flannel; yellow, turquoise and black embroidery silks; two small circles of card.

Embroider the outside felt first. Quarter the length of the felt and mark the places with three 2.5 cm (1") crosses in contrasting cotton (Fig 19). On these crosses, starting from the outside of each line, embroider fly stitches to the centre in black embroidery silk. In each angle put three single chain stitches in turquoise with a small straight stitch in yellow between each chain stitch and four small yellow straight stitches forming a cross in the centre (Fig 20). At each end, and in between these embroidered motifs, work a line of yellow chain stitch starting and finishing 1.25 cm (½") from the edge, with a row of black running stitches each side of it. Whip the running stitches with turquoise silk.

Sew a rectangle of flannel at one end of the white felt. Place both pieces of felt together with right sides outside and sew together with stab stitch in black silk. (Stab stitch is done by inserting the needle at right angles from back to front and then from front to back.)

In the centre of the card and felt circles punch a small hole (Fig 21). Work a 2 cm (¾") larger circle of yellow chain stitch round it with a small yellow straight stitch from the centre of each chain towards the edge. Oversew a red and a white circle together with a card circle in between, turn the circle over and do a second row of oversewing to cross over the first row.

Make a cord 38 cm (15") long from black and yellow embroidery silk. To do this, take four lengths of each colour 76 cm (30") long, and tie the ends. Put one end over a hook, put a pencil through the other end and twist. Or get someone to help you, twist your pencils in opposite directions and you will make your cord twice as quickly. When the twist is fairly taut, put both ends together, hold the middle and let it twist into a cord. Tie the two ends tightly about 2.5 cm (1") from the end, tie a second time just below the first one and make a tassel.

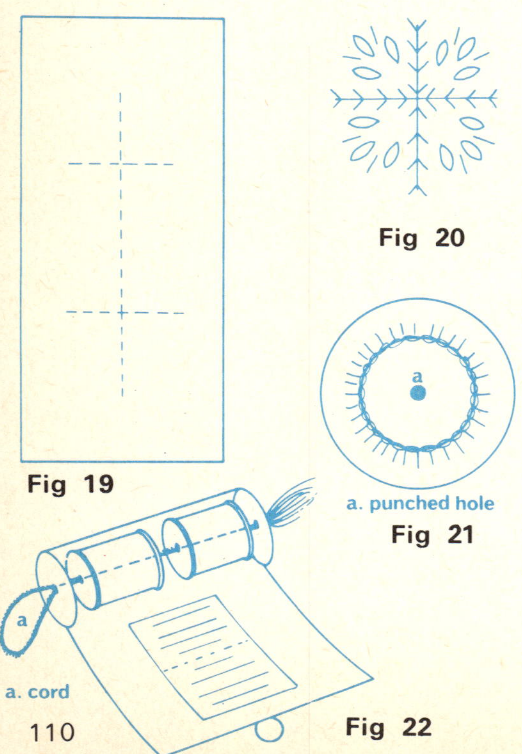

Fig 19

Fig 20

Fig 21

Fig 22

Thread the double end of cord through one circle from the red side, thread it through the two reels of cotton, and then through the second circle keeping the red side outside (Fig 22). Oversew the rectangle to the circles for about ¾ of the circumference.

In the middle of the opposite end work a buttonhole loop in black silk and sew a yellow button on the case to fasten it.

A drawstring bag in felt

Made in red felt lined with red and white checked gingham, on a circular base, this bag is embroidered round the lower part with a design based on a circle and a square. It measures 28 cm (11½") on a 15 cm (6") base. Made in a smaller size, in a pastel shade and embroidered with sequins and pearls, it would make a lovely party or theatre bag.

For one this size you will need:

A piece of felt measuring 44 cm (17½") square, a piece of gingham 49 cm by 47 cm (19½" by 18½"), a 15 cm (6") circle of thick card; embroidery silks (here they are black, white, green, yellow); red silk for a cord; some red sewing cotton.

Cut a rectangle of felt 44 cm by 29 cm (17½" by 11½") and one of gingham 47 cm by 31.5 cm (18½" by 12½"), this for the main bag.

Mark the 44 cm (17½") width of felt into three equal spaces with lines of tacking stitches. Mark this width on thin paper and in this space draw the design of square and circle. The square measures 4 cm (1½") and the circle 5 cm (2").

Pin the paper in one of the spaces and transfer the design to the felt with running stitches in contrasting cotton taken through the paper and the felt. Your embroidery will cover the running stitches.

The square has a line of yellow chain stitch double-threaded with black silk, three yellow chain stitches in a line from each corner with five black single chain (lazy daisy) stitches round them (Fig 23a).

The circle has a ring of green chain stitch whipped with white silk, with single white stitches raying out from the edge (Fig 23b). The centre of the circle is filled with five rows each way of long green chain stitch, forming squares, couched down at each join with white silk. Repeat this design in the other two spaces.

Fig 23a

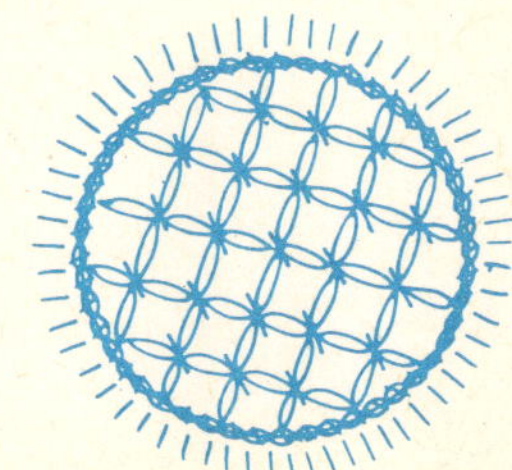

Fig 23b

Make 1.25 cm (½″) turnings on both long sides of the gingham and join the side seams on the wrong side. Oversew the side seams of the red felt, matching up the line of embroidery. Sew the lining into the felt tube at top and bottom edges, keeping seam to seam.

With red embroidery silk sew two lines of running stitches 4.5 cm (1¾″) and 6 cm (2¼″) from the top edge.

Make a small slit in the lining between these lines and oversew all round the slit to make an eyelet hole.

Make a cord from the red embroidery silk and thread it through the hem, tying the ends and fringing them into a tassel.

Trace round the card base on the wrong sides of the remaining pieces of felt and gingham, and cut them out, allowing a little extra on the felt for the thickness of the card and an extra 1.25 cm (½″) all round the gingham for turnings. Snip round the gingham circle and turn down on the pencil line. Pin it on to the wrong side of the felt and oversew about halfway round. Slide in the card circle and complete the oversewing. Pin the base of the bag round the circle and oversew the two together.

Fig 25

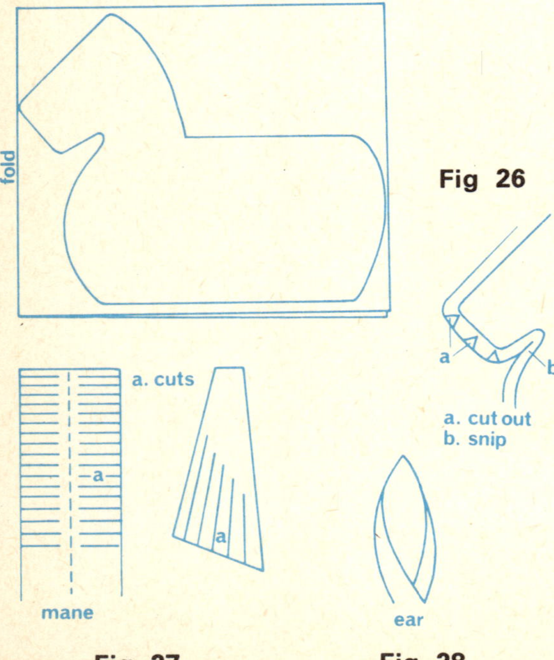

Fig 27

Fig 28

Cushions for children

A horse cushion

He is soft and cuddly to hug, is just as soft to lean against, or rest your head on, and can be made very bright and gay in almost any kind of firm material, gingham, linen weave or wool. Here, he is made in white cotton material spotted with green spots and little black stars. His mane, tail and features are in black felt, or could be in Vilene.

You will need:

A piece of material 38 cm by 71 cm (15″ by 28″); black and white felt or bonded interlining; some kapok or other soft stuffing; sewing cotton.

Fold the material in half to measure 38 cm by 35 cm (15″ by 14″) with the right sides inside. Trace round the template (Fig 24) on to one side of the folded material (Fig 25).

Tack round the outside edge of the shape, and machine carefully, or sew in back stitch all round the pencil line, leaving some of the bottom edge open for stuffing.

Trim off the edges close to the stitching, snip 'v's in all rounded edges and snip into any corners, at the neck particularly (Fig 26). Turn it inside out and press the seams flat.

Stuff it with kapok or chosen stuffing, softly and evenly.

Make small turnings on the bottom open edge and sew it up either with ladder stitch or with oversewing (which is not so neat).

Cut two 2.5 cm (1″) long ovals in white with a circle of black (drawn round a ½p piece) placed off centre on them, and sew on each side of the face near to the top of the head and pointing to the chin.

Sew on an oblong of black for a nose.

For the mane, cut a strip of felt 30 cm by 7.5 cm (12″ by 3″) and cut a fringe on each long side (Fig 27). Fold it in half and sew it on to the back seam, starting on the forehead opposite the eyes, and finishing at the bottom of the neck.

The tail is a triangular-shaped piece 10 cm (4″) long and 7.5 cm (3″) wide tapering to 2.5 cm (1″). Cut it in a fringe from the wide end to the narrow end and sew it in place.

The ears are triangles 7.5 cm by 5 cm (3″ by 2″), the 5 cm (2″) being the base. Fold the two corners to lap over in the middle of the base (Fig 28) and sew on near the top of the

body cut 2
allow 1.25 cm (½") extra all round for turnings
ear
cut 2
nose
cut 1
eye
cut 1
cut 1
Fig 24

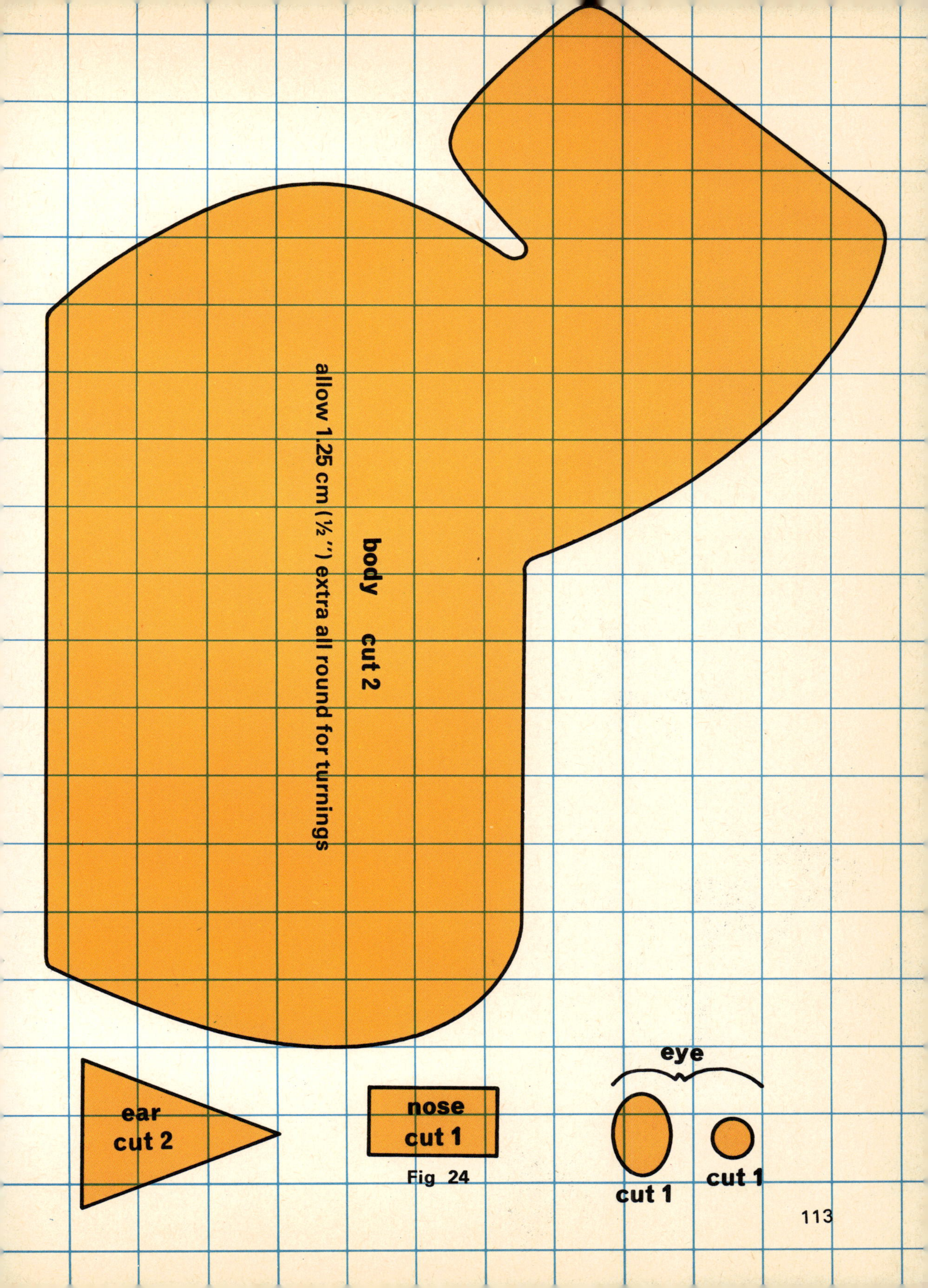

Fig 30

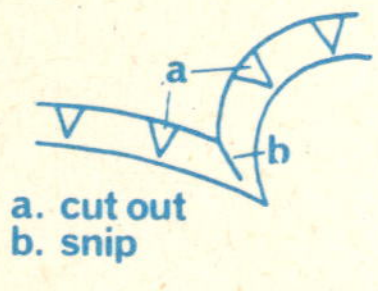

Fig 31

Fig 32

head, pointing upwards, again using ladder stitch and sewing them on both sides. Keep the ears upright as you sew them and they will then stay upright.

Bridle and reins of felt can be added if it is going to be a toy rather than a cushion.

A cat cushion

Fat and comfortable-looking, with a happy grin on her face, she is a cuddly cat to play with and also very nice to lean against.

You will need:

45 cm (½ yd) of 90 cm (36″) wide red and white plaid gingham, but any bright cotton-type material would be suitable; black felt or interlining for features; kapok or other soft stuffing material; black silk for whiskers; sewing cotton.

Fold the material in half with the right side inside, and trace round the template (Fig 29) of the cat; the tail template will fit in the space over the back (Fig 30).

Tack the shape together outside the pencil line, and machine or back-stitch round the pencil lines on each shape, leaving open the narrow end of the tail and some of the bottom edge of the cat. Trim off edges close to the stitching, snip 'v's out of all curves and snip into any corners close up to the stitching (Fig 31). Turn it inside out. Press all the seams flat, carefully pushing out the corners of the ears.

Stuff the body smoothly and softly, and sew up the opening with ladder stitch. Stuff the tail with small pieces of kapok to keep it smooth and flat rather than round. Sew it on at the back, curling it round to the side and fastening it in place with invisible stitches.

Cut a shield shape in black and sew it in the middle of the face with two lines of black chain stitch curling from the bottom of it for her smiling mouth. Long stitches in black from each curve will be her whiskers (Fig 32). Cut two long black ovals with pointed ends for the eyes, with a green circle in the centre fastened with a vertical bar of black stitching. Sew the eyes on at an angle, slanting in towards the nose.

A bright-coloured ribbon tied round her neck with a big bow will make her look a real pet.

body
cut 2
allow 1.25 cm (½″) extra all round for turnings
eye
cut 2
nose
cut 1
eye
cut 2
Fig 29

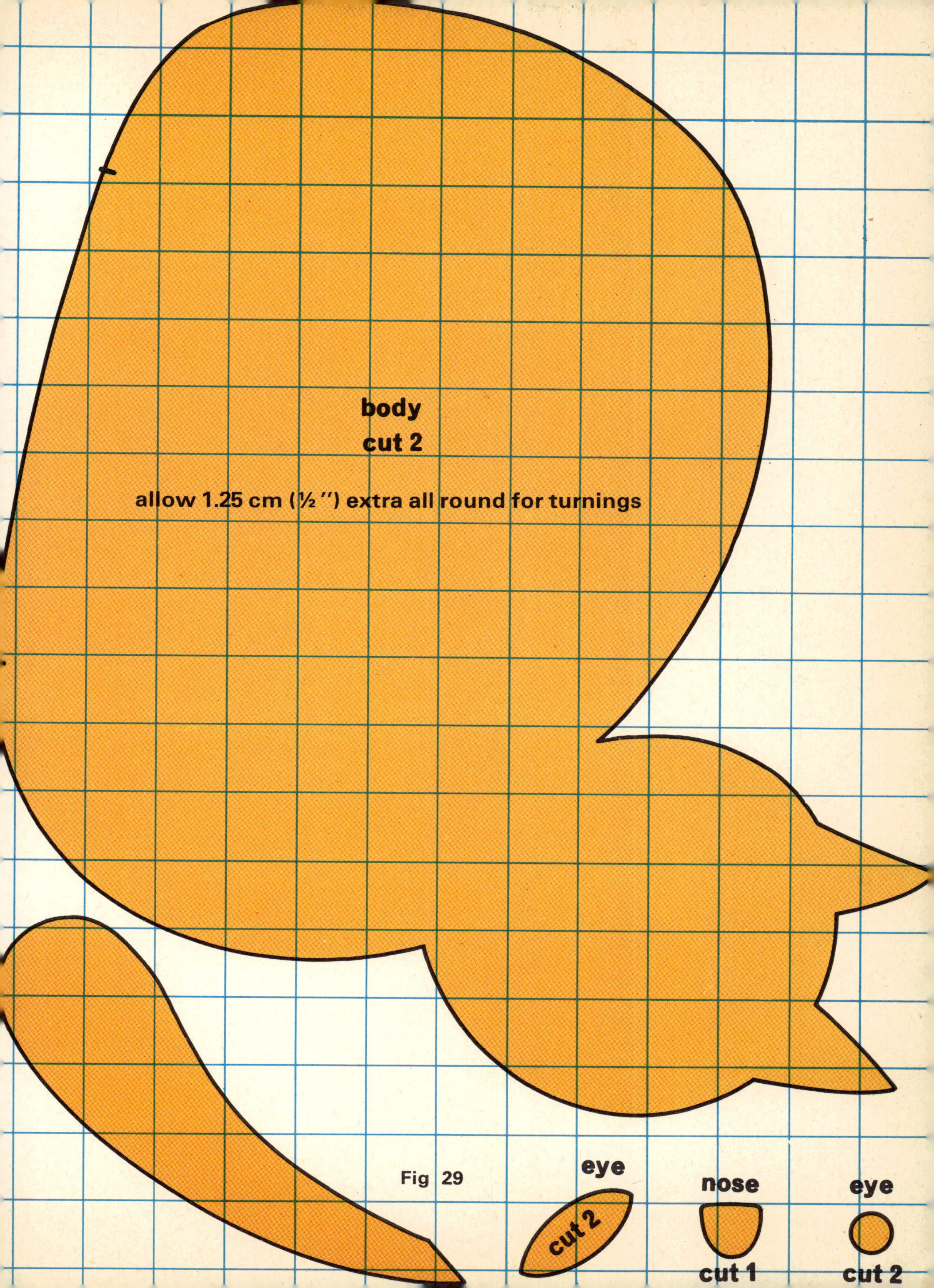

A lion cushion

A special cushion for a special person, a lovable, amiable lion like the one in ***The Wizard of Oz.*** Make him in gay colours in felt, cotton or velvet, patterned or plain. The actual cushion base is made of two square pieces of felt. The lion face can be worked straight on to one of these pieces for the front of the cushion, if the colour of it is suitable, and the back need not be the same colour. Or, you can make the face on a separate piece of material and sew it on to the front piece of the cushion. The lion's face is an oval shape, slightly wider at the top than the bottom, rather like an egg, in fact.

You will need:

Two pieces of felt 38 cm (15'') square; (40.5 cm (16'') square if other material is used to allow for turnings); scraps of material for features; two pieces of tawny-coloured felt or fabric for the mane, each piece measuring 61 cm by 11 cm (24'' by 4½''); a little kapok; some embroidery silks; a length of cord; some matching cotton.

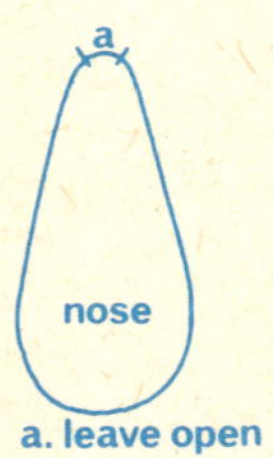

Fig 33

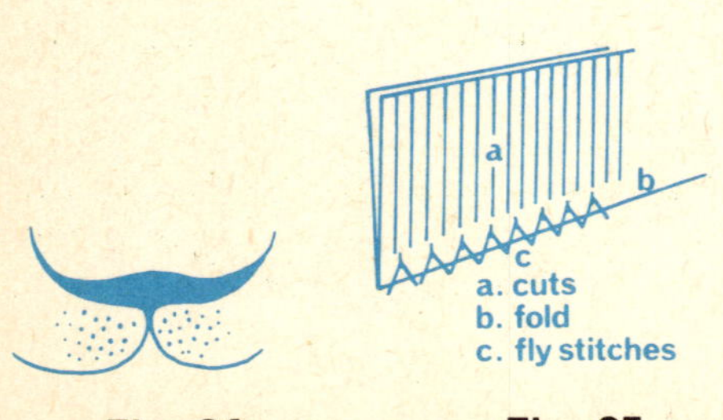

Fig 34

Fig 35

Nose

Cut out a long thin oval (Fig 33), broader at the base, for the nose, and sew it in the middle of the face, leaving about 5 cm (2'') open at the top, thin end. Through this opening gently push in a little kapok or other soft stuffing, to pad out the nose – it should be flat rather than rounded. Sew down the opening.

Eyes

For the eyes cut two thin ovals, pointed at each end, in white felt and two similarly-shaped smaller ovals in orange felt to fit in the centre of these for the eyes. Sew them together with an upright bar of whipped chain stitch in black silk. Sew the eyes in position slanting in towards the nose.

Nostrils

Cut the shaped piece for the nostrils in black and sew on at the lower end of the nose (Fig 34). Sew two curved lines for the mouth in whipped chain stitch or whipped stem stitch. Work some little seed stitches in each curve of the mouth.

Mane

Fold each long piece of felt in half lengthways and tack it all along the fold. Cut the two edges along the entire length into a narrow fringe (Fig 35). Pin it on round the face with the fringe spreading outwards, starting from the chin and overlapping on the forehead, the front piece of the overlap lower to give added thickness to the top mane. Sew down the length of the fold with single fly stitches, taking each stitch about 6 mm (¼'') up into the fold.

Work in a few whiskery straight stitches over the eyes.

If the cushion is made up as a 38 cm (15'') square, you will have the corners showing round the face. Trim these off if you do not like them, but the cushion pad which goes inside the cover must then have this same shape.

If felt has been used, tack the back and front together with right sides outside and join them together with crossed oversewing in contrasting colour embroidery silk, or lay a cord along over the join and couch it down.

If material is used, then make 1.25 cm (½'') turnings all round the edge and tack them together. Finish this off in the same way as for the felt lion.

A nursery cushion of felt pictures

These little felt pictures (see p 107) could easily be framed and hung up on the wall in a frieze, but here they have been sewn on to a linen cushion and would give much pleasure to a small child.

You will need:

90 cm (1 yd) of 90 cm (36″) wide crash or linen; a 46 cm (18″) square of felt; some pieces of felt in various sizes and colours for the actual pictures. The engine picture needs red, yellow, black, blue, white felt, the ark needs, in addition, pale blue, flesh, green felt and the sailing ship needs fawn felt as well; matching sewing cottons; yellow wool or cord for couching.

If you are making pictures to hang up, cut the big piece of felt into four equal squares, but for the cushion, mark it into four equal squares with contrasting tacking.

The engine has been split up into separate templates (Fig 36) for body, tender, coal, wheels and smoke—this is an old-fashioned steam engine.

Trace round the templates on to the wrong side of the felt with a very sharp pencil, using red felt for the engine, blue felt for the tender, black felt for coal, white felt for smoke and yellow felt for wheels. Place all the pieces in position before sewing, so that the finished whole will be in the centre of its square.

Sew the engine first, then the tender, coal, wheels and smoke, sewing with very small stitches in the same colour as the felt being sewn. Spokes for the wheels are straight stitches in black silk.

The template for the boat is cut from a 10 cm (4″) square. Use Fig 37 as a guide for cutting. The two corner pieces are the sails and the middle part the boat.

Trace the pieces on to their felts—the boat is fawn felt, the sails pale blue felt and yellow felt, and the pennant red felt. Again place all the pieces in position before sewing. Sew on the boat first.

The mast is several strands of orange embroidery silk couched down with contrasting silk. Place a sail each side of it and the pennant flying from the top of the mast.

The ball is a 15 cm (6″)-diameter circle cut into eight equal pieces and these used as templates to cut four royal blue felt and four pink felt segments (Figs 38a and 38b).

Before cutting up the circle, place it in the centre of the background square and mark round its edge with running stitch in contrasting cotton. This will be a useful guide for placing the segments so that they fit together exactly. Sew them in place in alternate colours, checking each one so that it takes up only its own space and no more, otherwise the last segment to be placed may have to overlap and that would spoil the effect.

When all are sewn, couch down round the edge some strands of matching pink embroidery silk.

The ark with Mr and Mrs Noah is again cut in sections to make the templates. Boat, ark and roof are separate and the figures are cut into body, face and hat, plus apron for Mrs Noah (Fig 39). Trace them on to the wrong side of the felt and place the pieces in position when cut.

Sew the red ark first, having cut a doorway and three windows in it. Then sew the boat and roof, the boat royal blue and the roof green.

Mr and Mrs Noah stand on each side of the ark, with one of the animals (it need not be a giraffe; it can be your own favourite animal) poking its head out of the door, probably hoping it is dinner time!

Sew all the pieces with matching cotton. Transparent nylon thread would be very useful for sewing this many-coloured kind of picture.

To make up the cushion, fold the linen in half and machine together the two sides, leaving open the two selvedge sides. Turn it inside out and press open the seams. Place the felt square on to it and pin it all round the edge, keeping it flat and trimming off any surplus felt. Tack it in place with small matching stitches.

Couch down yellow cord or strands of yellow wool across the middle from side to side each way, forming a cross to divide the pictures.

Finish it off by couching cord or wool all round the outside edge of the cushion to cover the tacking stitches, and taking the couching stitches (oversewing) through the cushion edge and the felt. Finish off the corners with loops of cord or small tassels of fringed wool.

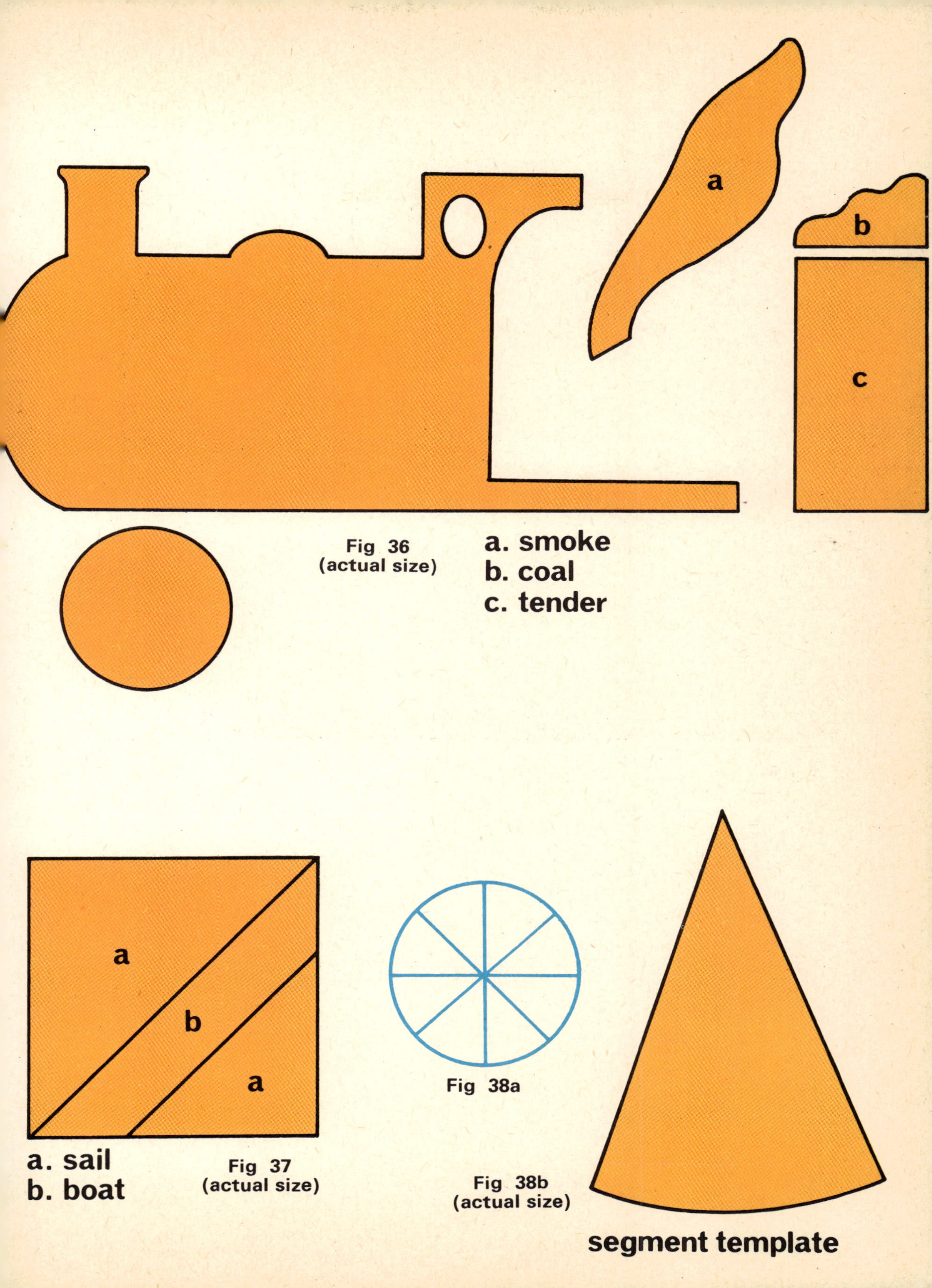

Fig 36 (actual size)

Fig 37 (actual size)

Fig 38a

Fig 38b (actual size)

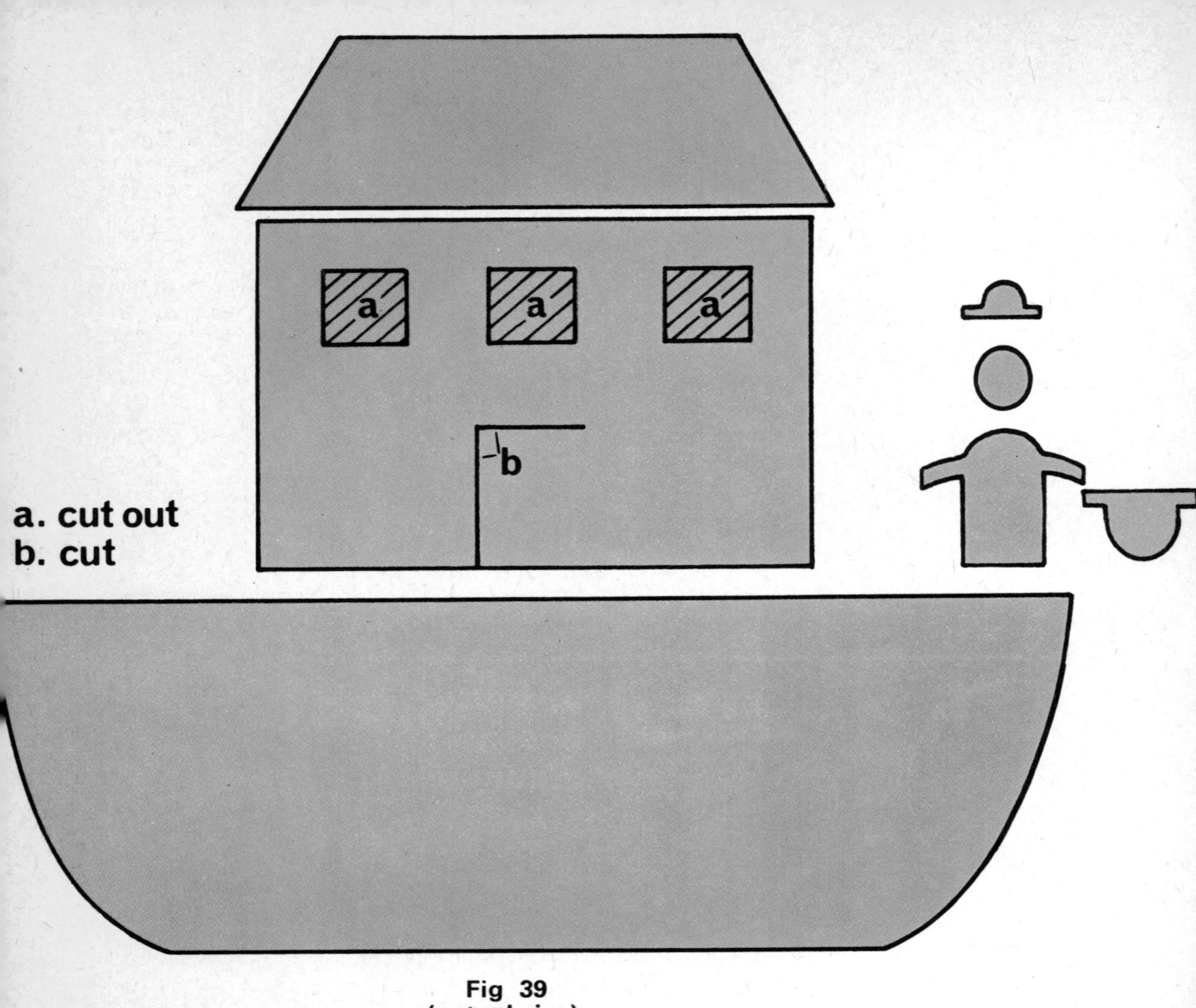

Fig 39
(actual size)

A Bonzo hound

He can be made from almost any kind of material, if it is fairly firm in weave, and can even be a patchwork of several pieces, if they are all the same thickness.

This Bonzo has the body in one pattern, head and tail in another, and the under gusset of a quite different pattern and colour (Fig 40). His ears are in plain material or felt, he measures 61 cm (24") from nose to tail and stands 25 cm (10") high.

You will need:

Material for making; kapok for stuffing; cotton for sewing.

Draw the pattern on to thin card and use it as a template. Do all the tracing on the wrong side.

If your material is big enough, you can cut head, body and tail in one piece for each side. If you are cutting each side in three parts, then place head, tail and side body templates on the folded material and cut two of each. The under gusset is of the legs from a curved line stretching from under the chin to under the tail. Cut two under gussets, four ears, two ovals for eyes, and a circle of 5 cm (2") diameter for his nose.

Machine or back-stitch all pieces together on the pencil lines on the wrong side. Stitch a tail piece on to each side piece, and a head piece on to the neck of the side pieces. Trim some of the surplus material and press the seams flat.

Place the two bodies together with right sides inside, matching neck and tail seams and sew the head and back seam, starting at the front of the neck, round the head and down the back, along both sides of the tail and finishing there. Trim and press open the seams.

Sew the curved seam of the under gusset on the wrong side. Pin it to the side pieces with the right sides together, starting at the feet. Sew round all the legs, leaving the under-body seams open on each side. Press open the seams. Turn it inside out.

Stuffing is done through the under-body openings and care must be taken not to split the seams as the openings are not very big. Stuff the head, pushing the stuffing well into the seams and corners of nose and mouth and packing it as firmly as possible without pulling the stitches. Stuff the tail with small pieces, pushing it well into the pointed end. Fill the legs and then the body, packing stuffing well into the root of the tail and the tops of the legs to keep them firm. Sew up the openings with ladder stitch.

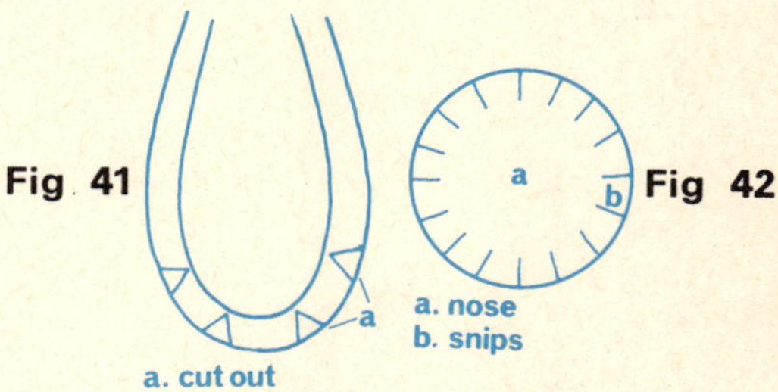

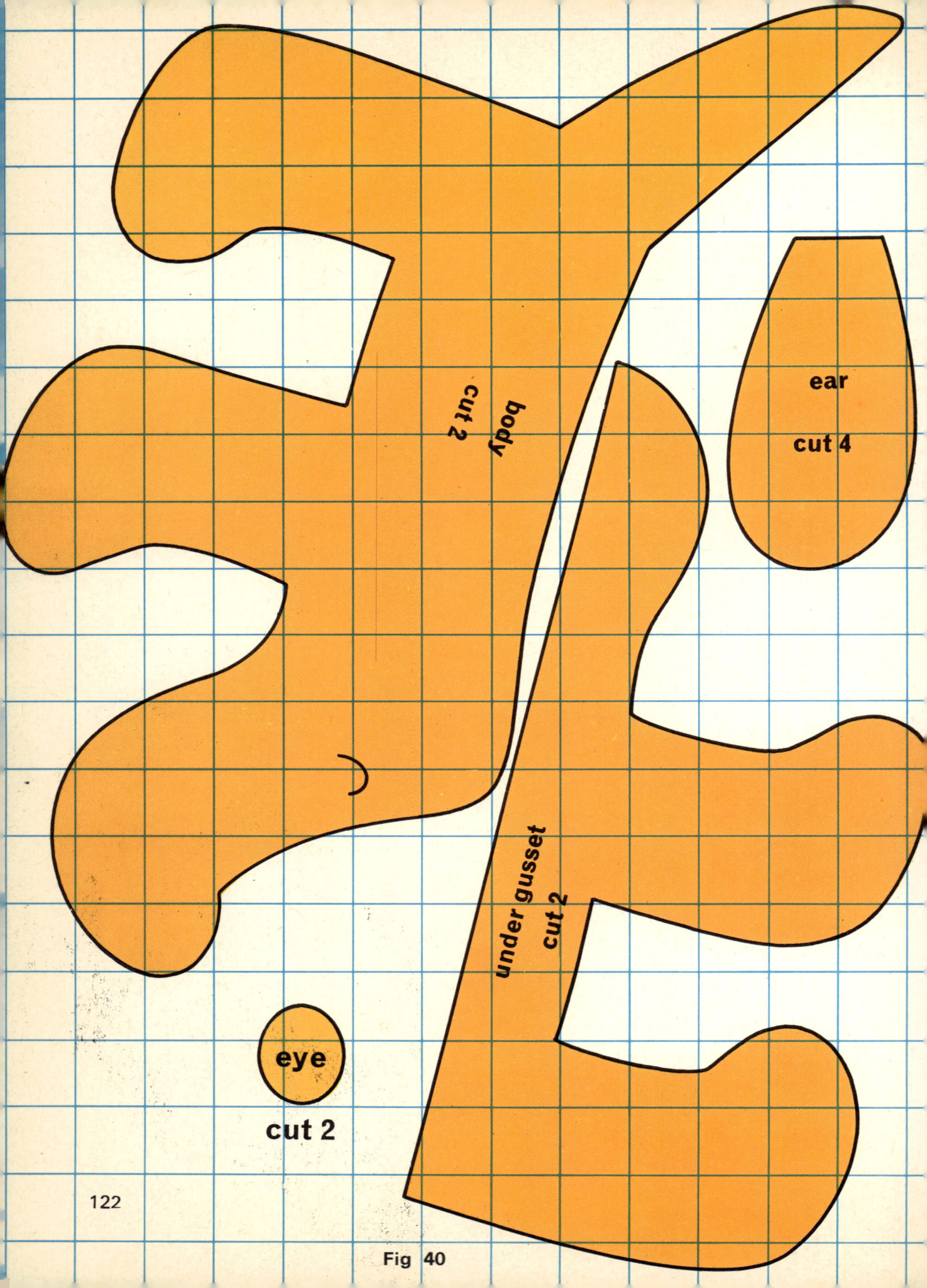

Fig 40

Machine together two ear pieces for each ear, trim off surplus turnings, snip out 'v's on the curves and turn it inside out. Stuff them sparingly, to give only a slight padded effect, turn in the raw edges at the top and sew on to the head near the top and slanting slightly to the back (Fig 41). Sew on the two eye ovals.

Snip the edges of the circle for the nose, gather up the snipped edges, put a ball of stuffing in the centre and sew it on the point of the nose with ladder stitch (Fig 42).

There he is, patiently waiting for a walk, or his dinner, or both.

A little girl's needlework box

This embroidered box (see p 125), worked with some of the aids to needlework, would make a lovely present for a little girl who likes to sew—all her cottons, embroidery silks, scissors, needles and pins fitting into a colourful box and ready for her to use. It is made from rectangles of thick card covered with felt, the outside of royal blue and lined with pale blue.

You will need:

Two pieces of card measuring 21.5 cm by 12.5 cm (8½" by 5") for top and base; two pieces 21.5 cm by 5 cm (8½" by 2") for the long sides; two pieces 12.5 cm by 5 cm (5" by 2") for the short sides; a piece of royal blue felt 36.5 cm by 27.5 cm (14½" by 10¾"); a piece of pale blue felt 36.5 cm by 27.5 cm (14½" by 10¾"); four short lengths of coloured embroidery silks; some fine silver metal-thread; 24 very small hooks, size 00; 12 very small shaped eyes; 16 size 00 press studs; 16 small silver beads; dark blue sewing cotton.

Cut both pieces of felt as shown in Fig 43. Each of the pieces will be 3 mm (⅛") larger than the corresponding card shapes, this to allow for the thickness of the card.

Embroider one of the large pieces of dark blue for the top of the box. Mark the diagonals from corner to corner on it (Fig 44), and across the middle from side to side, with tacking stitches in contrasting cotton, on the right side. Sew a 1.25 cm (½") pearl button in the centre and around it a ring of 'eyes' with the loops of them nearest to the button (Fig 45). Mark a 6.5 cm (2½") diameter circle with contrasting running stitches, on the right side, and from its edge sew sixteen 1.25 cm (½") long

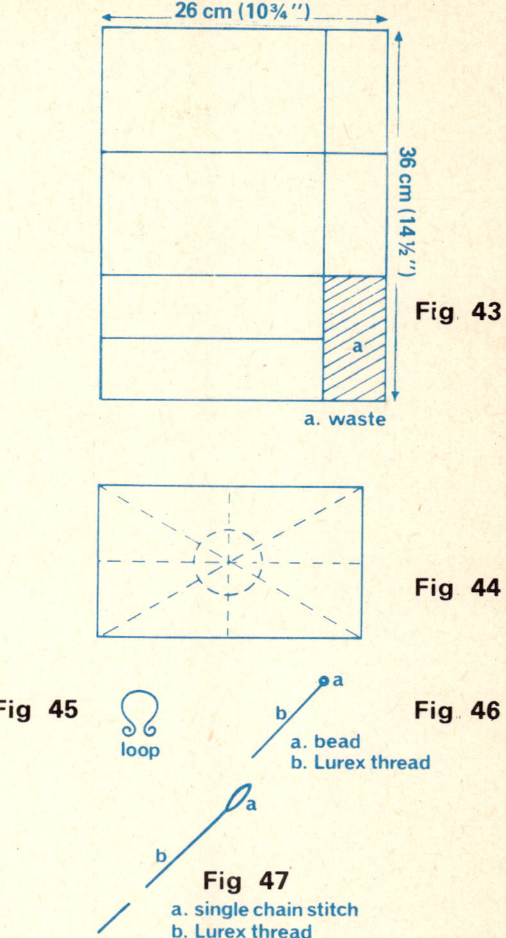

Fig 43

Fig 44

Fig 45

Fig 46

Fig 47

stitches pointing towards the centre, in fine silver metal-thread, and sew a silver bead on the circle at the end of each one to simulate pins (Fig 46).

Place the template of the scissors at the sides of the box shape between the diagonals, with the points towards the centre. Outline the template in tiny running stitches in contrasting cotton. The shapes are filled with close herring-bone stitch in fine silver metal-thread, and the finger rings in silver chain stitch.

At each corner sew the press studs, each in two pieces, six along the long side and two along the short side.

Sew a ring of six small hooks in each of the four spaces between the press studs and the ring of 'pins'. Sew them on with the hooks pointing outwards.

On the long sides in the centre space sew a long and a short stitch in line, in silver thread, diagonally, and a second lot of two stitches crossing it, with a single chain stitch at the outer end of each long stitch to simulate needles (Fig 47). In coloured embroidery silk work a trailing line of stem stitch from each 'eye' of the 'needle'. This completes the embroidery. (See Fig 48.)

Place a piece of pale blue felt behind the embroidered dark blue piece, with right side outside, and oversew three of the sides. Insert the appropriate card and oversew the remaining edge. Sew each of the other dark blue pieces to its lining, inserting the cards and sewing up the fourth sides. Oversew the four side pieces to the base, on the right side, and make into a box by sewing up the short sides on the corners. Oversew one long edge of the lid to the box.

Sew a pearl button in the middle of the front edge of the box, and make a buttonhole loop on the lid to fasten over it.

Fig 48

An embroidered trinket or jewel box

A very attractive effect can be obtained if the box is lined with a paler shade of the outside covering, which in a rich jewel colour sets off the glitter of sequin and fine metal-thread embroidery. The box in the picture is covered with purple felt and lined with pale mauve. It measures 15 cm by 7.5 cm (6″ by 3″) and is 5 cm (2″) deep. It is richly embroidered on lid and sides with beads, sequins and pearls and fine metal-thread.

You will need:

Felt in two colours; beads; sequins; pearls; fine metal-thread in one or two colours; embroidery silks; matching cotton; a length of fine silver or gilt cord; some thick card.

The six pieces comprising the box are made up separately and then all joined together.

Cut six pieces of thick card as follows:

Two pieces 15 cm by 7.5 cm (6″ by 3″) for top and base,
Two pieces 15 cm by 5 cm (6″ by 2″) for the long sides,
Two pieces 7.5 cm by 5 cm (3″ by 2″) for the short sides.

The corresponding pieces of felt must be cut slightly larger to allow for the thickness of the card. Allow an extra 3 mm (⅛″) on each piece for this.

Cut a second corresponding set of pieces from the lining felt.

Now embroider all the outside pieces except the piece for the base and embroider one lining piece for inside the lid.

For the top (Fig 49), on the wrong side of the piece of felt draw diagonal lines from corner to corner. Use a white pencil on dark colours. Tack along these lines in contrasting cotton, taking long stitches through to the right side.

The design is composed of concentric circles of embroidery with diagonal lines of embroidery stretching to the corners. Start in the centre with a big red sequin fastened down with silver thread. Outside this is a ring of twelve single chain (lazy daisy) stitches in bright turquoise silk with a bright blue bead between them touching the centre sequin. At the tip of each chain stitch sew a bright gold sequin with a small gold bead in between. A ring of bright pink chain stitch whipped with fine green metal-thread round them, and outside this a ring of emerald green shiny beads sewn closely together. A row of gold-coloured fly stitches with a pearl sewn at the tip of each point completes the circle, which should measure between 6 cm and 6.5 cm (2¼" and 2½") from side to side.

On each diagonal work 3.2 cm (1¼") of green stem stitch with a fly stitch at the end and five slanting stitches down each side. Sew a bright red sequin in the fly stitch and at the end of alternate side stitches.

The long front side

On the wrong side draw a line lengthways down the middle. Mark the middle of it, mark 2.5 cm (1") from each end and draw cross lines. Tack along these lines, again taking long stitches through to the right side.

In the centre piece sew a medium-size gold sequin with fine red metal-thread, and round it a row of ten bright pink single chain stitches. In between them sew emerald green bugle beads, and at the tip of them a bright blue sequin. At the tip of each sequin and each bugle bead sew a turquoise bead, and sew straight stitches of fine silver metal-thread spraying out all the way round (see Fig 50.)

Fig 49

Fig 50

The motif each side of the centre one has a silver sequin centre with eight silver metal-thread stitches round it. At the end of each stitch is sewn a small yellow bead with a turquoise bead in between the stitches.

The long strip for the back has three similar motifs on it. The middle one has a red sequin centre with eight fine silver metal-thread stitches round it, a turquoise bead at the end of each stitch and an emerald green one in between. The end ones differ in that they have gold sequin centres and silver beads in between the stitches.

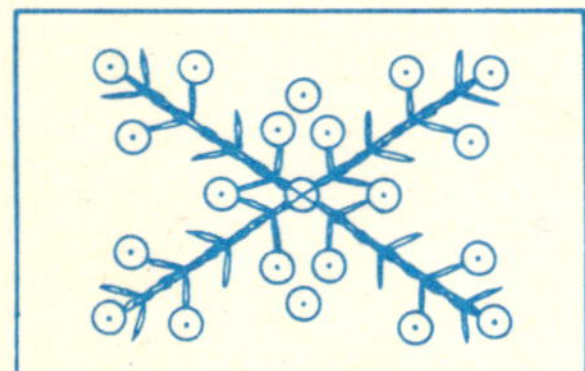

Fig 51

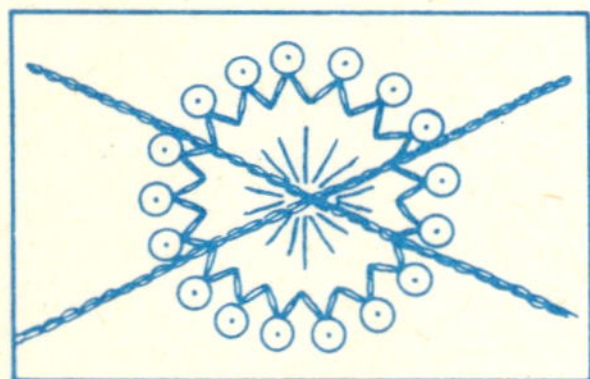

Fig 52

The two sides

Mark the diagonals as on the other pieces. Sew a bright green sequin in the centre. From the centre sew each diagonal in mauve stem stitch for 2.5 cm (1″) with a single fly stitch at the end and three slanting stitches each side. Sew gold sequins in each fly stitch and at the ends of alternate slanting stitches. Sew a red sequin between the two gold ones which come together in the wide angle (Fig 51).

On the mauve lining for the lid, embroider a flat design in silks and sequins. Mark the diagonals and embroider 7.5 cm (3″) on each in pink chain stitch whipped with fine emerald green metal-thread. From the centre, embroider straight stitches in fine red metal-thread in a sunburst design. In a circle 2 cm (¾″) radius from the centre embroider turquoise fly stitches and sew red and gold sequins alternately on each point (Fig 52).

Pair all the pieces with their lining pieces with right sides outside, and oversew three sides on each, insert the appropriate cards and sew up the fourth side.

Make up the box in the same way as the work box.

Sew a fine silver cord all round the top edge of the box, beginning at the centre of the back. Use an oversewing stitch, but put the needle through the strands of cord and not over the top of it, so that the effect of the cord will not be spoilt by the stitches. Overlap the cord slightly at the back and finish off securely.

In the same way, sew cord round the edge of the lid starting about 1.25 cm (½″) round the corner of the back edge, continuing round the side to the middle of the front edge. Here make a small loop for lifting the lid. Continue sewing, finishing off firmly about 1.25 cm (½″) round the back corner, and not sewing any cord along the back.

Sew the lid to the box with fishbone stitch, putting the needle each time between the strands of the cord and bringing it out first through the lid and then through the back of the box.

All decoration on a box of this kind must be done before any sewing together is attempted.

In working out designs for the embroidery, first make a plan of each piece, square it off and mark the diagonals. Using coloured pencils or felt-tip pens to denote sequins, beads and threads in the design will help to give some idea of the effect of the colour scheme.